NOTES FROM MY BIBLE

NOTES FROM MY BIBLE

FROM GENESIS TO REVELATIONS

BY

D. L. MOODY

Fredonia Books
Amsterdam, The Netherlands

Notes from My Bible:
From Genesis to Revelations

by
Dwight L. Moody

ISBN: 1-58963-956-1

Copyright © 2002 by Fredonia Books

Reprinted from the 1895 edition

Fredonia Books
Amsterdam, The Netherlands
http://www.fredoniabooks.com

All rights reserved, including the right to reproduce this book, or portions thereof, in any form.

In order to make original editions of historical works available to scholars at an economical price, this facsimile of the original edition of 1895 is reproduced from the best available copy and has been digitally enhanced to improve legibility, but the text remains unaltered to retain historical authenticity.

TO THE READER.

The power of anecdote and illustration to press home the truth into the hearts and minds of their hearers is largely utilized by preachers and teachers of to-day.

The occasion often happens, however, when an anecdote would put the text out of sight, and when some trite saying, some deep thought crystallized into a few words, would serve the preacher's purpose better, in order to flash light upon his subject.

During the course of my reading, I have always tried to gather "nuggets" by the way, and make a note of them on the margins and blank leaves of my Bible. I have found it to be a useful habit, preserving for use many seed-thoughts and apt sayings that otherwise would have escaped my memory.

"Notes from My Bible" is the harvest of many years gathering in this direction, and I want it to be distinctly understood that its contents are not claimed to be original. The flowers in this book have been culled from many gardens. I would be glad to give full credit to the men to whom I am indebted, by attaching their names to their sayings; but I found that this could be done only very partially, and therefore decided to omit names in every instance.

The arrangement of the book is simple. Over against the text is the thought or illustration. At the beginning of the books and chapters of the Bible is placed whatever has a general reference to that section. A number of miscellaneous outlines are added at the end of Revelation.

I take this opportunity of impressing upon you, reader, the advantage of making notes. Let this book serve you not only as a storehouse, but also as a stimulus. Whether you are minister or layman, you will find that you will grow more deeply interested in your Bible day by day if you follow the course of making notes of sayings similar to those contained in this volume, of outline sermons, and of anything that helps to light up some well-known truth and fasten it in the memory. It is a good thing to be ready with new thoughts to present the old truths of the Bible.

God grant that this book may be very helpful to you.

THE BIBLE.

This Book will keep you from sin, or sin will keep you from this Book.

> Here search, and great shall be your store:
> Here drink, and you shall thirst no more.

Sir Walter Scott, on his deathbed, said, "There is but one Book," and asked his friends to read the Bible.

Dean Stanley used to peruse a book first for the story, second for the thought, third for the style — three separate readings. A good rule to follow in reading the books of the Bible

There is not a verse in the Bible where I am told merely to "read" it, but many verses where I am exhorted to study, to search. If I search, I will always find something new.

In reading the word of God, I am not only to arrive at comprehension, but also at appropriation.

NOTES FROM MY BIBLE

GENESIS.

Adam illustrates Human nature.
Cain " The carnal mind.
Abel " The spiritual mind.
Enoch " Communion.
Noah " Regeneration.
Abraham " Faith.
Isaac " Sonship.
Jacob " Service.
Joseph " Suffering and glory.

THE BOOK OF BEGINNINGS.

Creation, chapter 1.
Origin of Human Race, 1:26.
" " Sabbath, 2:2, 3.
" " Marriage, 2:18, 21–24.
" " Sin and Death, 2.16, 17; 3:4–7.
" " Sacrifice (grace), 3:21.
" " Covenant Promises, 8:20-22; 9:1–17.
" " Nations, Races, and Tongues, 10:11.
" " The Chosen People, 12:1–3.

Genesis 1. How the world was made.
Genesis 3. How lost.
John 1. How redeemed.
Rev. 20. How to be reconstructed.

Gen. 1. Seven stages of creation, illustrative of stages in the new creation: chaos, brooding of the Spirit light, life, growth, fruit, rest.

Creation, light, separation, growth, fruit-bearing.

God creating, moving, speaking, observing, calling, dividing, blessing.

"It was so"— seven times.

"It was good"— seven times.

"God'— Elohim — thirty-one times; in every verse but five.

Verse 1. God the Father.
" 2. God the Spirit.
" 3. God the Son (See John 8:12.)
" 3. Conversion
" 7. Separation.
" 12. Fruit-bearing.

1: 1. The Bible opens without an apology.

"I do not know anything more difficult to believe than just the first verse of the Bible. If we master this verse, anything else that happened in the heavens or in the earth which God created will not stumble us."

"*Through faith* we understand that the worlds were framed by the word of God." Heb. 12:3.

God first came down to create, then to save. To create, God had only to speak; to redeem, he had to suffer. He made man by His breath; He saved him by His blood. Rom. 5:9.

26. In bearing God's image, man could bear God's rule.

He who gave His image to us must of necessity like to see His image in us.

1:26. Man is the excellency of the creature; the saint is the excellency of the man.

2:2. God rested on the seventh day, yet he had not made woman! In making her, he seems to have begun again. O woman, love thy maker!

4. "Lord God"— in the Hebrew, Jehovah Elohim

8. Eden is our home; we are exiles now.

9. Not the tree of knowledge in general, but the test-tree, by which Adam would gain the knowledge of good and evil.

The tree of knowledge has often been planted and has flourished where the tree of life never grew.

17. When all around was life, God spake of death. Now, when all is death, God speaks of life.

18. How does God propose to meet loneliness? For man to be alone means suicide; for two men together, homicide (Cain slew Abel); the only chance of keeping society together is by the marvelous influence of *woman*.

21. In forming woman, God did not take a part from his head to dispute his supremacy, nor from his feet, lest he should despise her, but from near his heart so that he should love and cherish her.

So much is being done for us when we are unconscious of it!

3:1. God tests — the devil tempts.

God made man for his own glory, but he joined the devil and became a rebel.

Satan began with the woman because novelty and

mystery appeal more to her than to man. Also because woman can influence man more than anyone else.

"Every"— R. V. reads "any." Thus Satan lies.

If woman originally tempted man away from God, now she tempts him back.

Satan's three lies are still in the world —
1. God does not love you, for He has forbidden some things.
2 Ye shall not surely die.
3. Ye shall be as gods.

3 : 3. Man lost life by believing the devil, and regains it by believing the Son of God. We must rise at the point where we fell

"Lest ye die"— spiritual and natural death which would begin the very moment they eat of the fruit, but which would not be completed on that day. But in both soul and body the process was begun: they had passed the line that separated life and death. See Rom. 5 : 12.

4. The first lie!
5. Tempted to an upward fall!

Satan's words are ambiguous. Eve's eyes were opened and she did know good and evil, but the experience was more bitter than she expected. They saw, not visions of glory, but their own nakedness and sinfulness.

6. { "Good for food" — "The lust of the flesh."
{ "Pleasant to the eyes"—"The lust of the eyes."

"To make one wise"— "The pride of life "
1 John 2 16

Satan's pills are sugar-coated.

We are sons and daughters of a woman who was too curious.

3 : 9. God's first question — "Where art thou?" Man asked the first question in the New Testament — " Where is he?" See Matt. 2:2.

God's second question was — "Where is Abel thy brother?" Ch. 4:9.— Human responsibility.

"Where art thou?" *Hiding from God.* Why? From fear.

Reasons for fear —
   a. God s holiness. Ex. 3 6; Isa. 6; Rev. 1 17.
   b. Man's sinfulness Job 42:5, 6.

Behind what to hide?

It is impossible — Prov. 28. 13; Amos 9·2-4; Ps. 139: 7-12, Jonah 1 3.

Only one safe hiding-place—Jesus. Rev. 6. 12-17.

10. Men hide behind : —
   a. False hopes.
   b. Indifference.
   c. Excuses.
   d. Self-righteous acts.
   e. Innocence.
   f. Ignorance.

14. The first curse!

The serpent is the only animal with a bony skeleton that goes upon its belly.

3:16. Seven things that came by the Fall and have their complement in Christ. —

By the Fall —   In Christ: —
- V. 16. Pain   Isa 53.11; Acts 2:24.
- V. 16. Subjection.   Gal. 4:4.
- V. 17. The Curse.   Gal. 3:13.
- V. 17. Sorrow.   Isa. 53:3.
- V. 18. Thorns   Matt. 27:29.
- V. 19. Sweat.   Luke 22:44.
- V 19. Death.   Phil 2:8.

"Night has fallen upon the guilty pair, but in the night there are stars that lead on to a manger, a child, a Saviour."

17. "Cursed is the ground" The ground teaches many lessons —
  a. The land is the true wealth of a nation, and other trades and professions depend on it.
  b. You get nothing out of it except by labor.
  c. It teaches patient industry and hopefulness: there is no use getting mad with it. So spiritual cultivation takes time. See James 5:7; 2 Cor. 9:6; Gal. 6:7; Eccl. 11:6.

18. Thorns — the curse of man, the crown of Christ.

20. The name "Eve" was not given until after the Fall.

21. First occasion of death and of blood — "Unto Adam also and to his wife did the Lord God make coats of skins. and clothed them."

GENESIS.

Before Adam fell, he was clothed in glory. Primarily, clothes are the trappings of guilt.

3 : 21, 23. Grace.

24. Government.

Man by sin closed one way. Jesus opened a new and living way.

Results of sin : —

3 : 8. Remorse ; alienation from God.

3 : 9. Discovery.

3 : 12, 13. Selfishness, blaming others.

3 : 16, 17. Sorrow.

3 : 19. Death.

4 : 1. When Eve bare Cain, she said — "I have gotten a man from the Lord." Cain's subsequent conduct showed that the Lord had very little to do with him.

Saint Augustine said he did not know but that his family would turn out bad, for in the family of

Adam	there was a murderous Cain.
Noah	a scoffing Ham.
Abraham	a persecuting Ishmael.
Isaac	a profane Esau.
David	an undutiful Absalom.
Elisha	a lying Gehazi.

Christ's disciples a traitorous Judas.

8. The first grave in the Bible was dug by a brother.

Abel was the first solo singer in heaven. The angels could not sing the song of redemption, of Moses and the Lamb He was the first saint in the church triumphant.

As Abel's body was the first that took possession of the earth, so his soul was the first that was translated to heaven.

4 : 9. Cain thought it was not his duty to be his brother's keeper, but did not consider it against his duty to be his brother's murderer.

10. Abel's blood demanded vengeance on the murderer; Christ's blood spoke mercy, atonement, and pardon.

Abel was a type of Christ, yet a contrast. His sheep died for him, but Christ died for his sheep. John 10 : 14.

13. Oh, the consequences of sin! We can best know sin by its results and effects. Note its evil effect on personal appearance, character, etc.

17. The first city established on earth.

5 : A chapter of nobodys.

"Names, nothing more. But such people are unjustly underestimated. The best part of human history is never written. Guy Fawkes was well known, but your honest father was unknown, six doors from his house. You do n't know where a flat road will lead to: Seth to Jared, then *Enoch!* Your son may be a big man yet. Methusalah was known for longest life, Blondin for walking a tight rope, but noblest deeds are often forgotten."

24. Enoch was one of the few men in the Bible against whom God had nothing.

The Path of Fellowship — with God. V. 24.
The Path of Holiness — before God. Gen. 17 : 1.
The Path of Obedience — after God. Deut. 13 : 4.

Walking with God is a condition of life consistently lived through years; e. g., Enoch, three hundred and sixty-five years. Not rapturous, occasional.

Chief characteristic — constant consciousness of God; e. g., husband and wife.

Character of life — (1) joyful. Ps. 16 : 11; (2) peaceful; (3) brave, because life is difficult. Ps. 118 : 6, 14.

How attained? Only by believers. (1) Remember God's promise to walk with us. Lev. 26 : 11, 12; (2) Keep out of our lives things that would offend God and break communion. Separate yourself from sin; e. g., Enoch, Noah. 2 Cor. 6 : 16, 17; (3) Wait upon God; cement the friendship in secret.

6 : 3. God's first warning: "My Spirit shall not always strive with man."

6. Sin has troubled God. Has it troubled you?

8. There are good men in the worst of times. Bad times test faith and virtue.

"God saw that the wickedness of man was great in the earth, and that every imagination of the thoughts of his heart was only evil continually. . . . But Noah found grace in the eyes of the Lord." Who would have looked for so fair a bird in so foul a nest?

7 : 1. The first "come" of the Bible is one of salvation — "Come thou and all thy house into the ark." So is the last "come"— "The Spirit and the bride say, Come. And let him that heareth say, Come. And let him that is athirst come. And whosoever will, let him take the water of life freely." Rev. 22:17.

A woman was once telling what a wonderful preacher she had. Some one objected, saying that if he were, more people would go to hear him "But," she asked, "were there many who went into the ark after Noah's preaching?"

The seven "forty days" of the Bible : —
  (1.) Forty days of sin and its judgment. Gen. 7 : 4, 12, 17.
  (2.) Forty days of law and mercy. Ex 24 : 18 ; 34 : 28.
  (3.) Forty days of faith and unbelief. Deut. 9 : 9 ; Num. 13 : 14.
  (4.) Forty days of human weakness and divine strength. 1 Kings 19 : 1–8.
  (5.) Forty days of repentance and forgiveness. Jonah 3.
  (6.) Forty days of conflict and victory. Luke 4 : 2.
  (7.) Forty days of redemption and glory. Acts 1 : 3.

16. The Lord shut Noah and his family in, and shut all others out.

8 : 20. Beautiful to think, that after the flood, there was a church before there was a house! But human

nature was the same. Destruction (for the sake of reform) was a failure as regards the survivors. Punishment can never regenerate the heart of man.

The second dispensation was founded on the doctrine of atonement. With sacrifices Noah took possession of the new world.

9 : 13. "I do set my bow in the cloud, and it shall be for a token of a covenant between me and the earth." Old forms may be put to new uses. The stars and the sand may become Abraham's family register. Cultivate the spirit of moral interpretation: then the rainbow will keep away the flood; the fowls of the air will save you from anxiety; the lilies of the field will assure you of tender care.

11 : 3. Our business is to build upon a right foundation, and in a right spirit. Beware of atheistic building. 1 Cor 3:10.

7. The Lord's ways of punishing and of fulfilling his purposes are many. Who would have thought of this means of scattering men — "Let us go down and there confound their language"?

Has your tower been thrown down? Was it honestly built? If so, remember, the foundation abideth forever. Continue to build and be assured of the final reward.

28. Ur of the Chaldees has been unearthed. It was the seat of a public library.

12 : 1. *Man-made and God-made plans.*
  11:3, 4. "Go to, let us make, . . . let us build,"
    — luck.
  12:1, 2. "Get thee out, . . . I will make," —
    God.
  The first was a failure: the second a success.
    Compare, Cain — Abel; Jacob — Israel; Saul
    — Paul.
  Gen. 11:3. They built Babel with artificial bricks.
  Ex. 20:25. God commanded the Israelites to build altars out of stone.
  God's calls are upward; Christianity ennobles.
  Abram was the minister of God to all around him.
    Had he wavered, the others would have been disorganized.

2. How did God fulfil his promise to Abram?

7. Abram was on the right road, so God's faithfulness followed him.

18. *a.* Reproof by the heathen for telling lies.
  b. The divine forbearance of human infirmity. God did not send Abram home in disgrace, but forgave his weakness.

13 : 4. Returning to first faith: from indifference, skepticism, iniquity, etc.

  12. "Lot pitched his tent toward Sodom." Always unsafe.

  12, 13. A great estate, but bad neighbors. So men take their families into a moral desert for the sake of a garden to play in.

14: A New Testament picture. We are all taken captives by Satan, but Christ recovers us.

15 : 6. First use of "believe," in the Bible.

17. The awful furnace — the cheerful lamp.
The furnace of conviction; the lamp of pardon.
The furnace of trial; the lamp of consolation.
The furnace of want; the lamp of prosperity.
The furnace of death; the lamp of glory.

16 : 9. "Submission" is a great Christian law, but we find it early in Genesis.

17 : 1. "The Almighty God" — EL SHADDAI.
See note to Gen. 5:24.

18 : 9. "Sarah thy wife." So Jesus called Zachæus unexpectedly by name.

14. Abraham took God at his word, and so he became the friend of God.

18. Abraham, in communion with God, knew, long before Lot himself, of the destruction of the city of Sodom.

23. God transcends man's reason, mocks at his speculation, but He will not violate his conscience. See 19 : 24; John 15 : 15.

32. Abraham ceased asking before God ceased giving.
A member of Parliament brought in a Temperance Bill into the House of Commons. It was rejected eighteen times, but on the nineteenth it passed, to his surprise.

19 : *Warning Angels.* — The Bible, the Holy Spirit, friends. Providence conscience.

NOTES FROM MY BIBLE.

19:37, 38. The Moabites and Ammonites became Israel's bitter enemies. The bitter fruit of backsliding.

21: Isaac born: opposition of Ishmael. The two natures in the believer.

    15. A soldier's canteen was once found with this on it: "Died for want of water!"

    19. Provision for the sinner's need. "I was brought low and He helped me."

22: 1. "Tempt"—rather, test. James 1:12.

    2. Calvary was a spur of Mount Moriah.

    13. The lamb was there, although they did not see it.

    16. Abraham withheld nothing, and God gave him everything.

23: 2. Sarah is the only woman whose complete age, death, and burial are recorded in Scripture.

    3. The first account of a funeral.

    9. The earliest money transaction on record.

24: A model servant:—
    True. Vs. 2, 35.
    Earnest. V. 33.
    Praying. V. 12.
    Single-eyed. V. 52.

The marriage of Isaac is the first in Scripture of which we have particulars. A long chapter is devoted to it.

    58. "I will go." Decide for yourself.

25 : 32. "Behold, I am at the point to die: and what profit shall this birthright do to me?" Did Esau mean by this that he had only a short time to live anyway? "Let us eat and drink, for to-morrow we die."

33. There was never any food, except the forbidden fruit, so dearly bought as this broth.

Esau was bad stock. See 26 : 34, 35.

26 : 34. A sin is sometimes aggravated (or the reverse) by the age of the sinner.

27 : 6. Jacob led astray by his mother!

The Deception of Isaac. "In solving this moral puzzle, do not forget that Jacob was divinely appointed to be the inheritor of the blessing (Gen. 25 : 23). His error was not in feeling the pressure of destiny, but in taking it into his own hands and pushing it. Rebekah knew Esau had done wrong (Gen. 26 : 35). So she wanted to make this straight perhaps."

21. Only one man in the whole Bible wanted to *feel*, and he was deceived.

23. It is a grand thing to want the blessing of the Lord, but a poor thing to get it by fleshly craft.

38. Esau wept because he had lost the blessing, not because he had sold his birthright. Men mourn for the evil that sin brings, not for the sin which brings the evil.

28 : 5. Isaac lived sixty-three years after Jacob left home, but he drops out of importance now. We cannot tell the end of a man's life from the beginning, or vice versa.

28 : 12. None of the angels on the ladder stood still.

Visions leading God-ward. See Gen. 48 : 3.

An answer to prayer. See Gen. 35 : 3.

{ For loss of country : "To thee will I give this land." V. 13.
For loss of friends : "I am with thee." V. 15.

15. "I will keep thee in all places whither thou goest," not only "whither I send thee."

"With thee" — companionship.

"Keep thee" — guardianship.

"Bring thee" — guidance.

29 : 25. How human Jacob was in his innocence! How forgetful of his own deception!

God spared Jacob : therefore I must not strike him. We may not know the whole story. In the meanest of us there is a soul meant for heaven.

31 : 47. Different names for the same thing.

49. Mabie thinks Jacob meant to make a clean cut with Laban here. "Separation" — getting clear of the worldly ties.

32 : 27. "What is thy name?" "My name is Money, Moderation in religion, Ananias, Frivolity, Lust, Uncleanness." How few can answer: "My name is Honesty, Principle, Purity."

31. Meyer once overheard a lady say his address was "lovely!" Did Jacob limp into the tent and say to Rachel he had had a "lovely" time with the angel? Rather was he not pale and serious?

On this side of eternity we shall never be perfect. Jacob limped.

Better limp to heaven than leap to hell.

33 : 9. "Enough"—the first man who ever said so. Christianity should be proved by being contented, not by being satisfied, with this world.

35 : This chapter recounts four burials:—
(1.) Jacob's idols. V. 4.
(2.) Nurse. V. 8.
(3.) Wife. V. 19.
(4.) Father. V. 29.

35 : 19. The first mention of Bethlehem. In the N. T. its first mention is in connection with the birth of Jesus. Matt. 2 : 1.

37 : 8. Fulfilled in Ch. 50:18. See Luke 19:14.

20. A plan is not right because it is easy. It is convenient to have a beast to blame.

39 : 3. Some of us have a skilful way of concealing our religion; not so Joseph.

5. It is Joseph who blesses the house of Potiphar. It is Jesus through whom we are blessed.

40 : 14. A touch of human nature.

God will answer your cry in His own good time.

41 : 8. The old school of thought was unable for the new difficulties of life.

46. It took thirteen years to fulfil Joseph's dream!

But it was a great dream, and God took time to work it out. The baker and butler had theirs answered in three days.

Thirteen years discipline for Joseph. But remember, God was now training a spoiled child.

42 : 1. Why did the sons tarry? Because the mention of "Egypt" brought back the memory of their sin, and they were afraid to go thither.

21. (1.) Conscience.
(2.) Memory.
(3.) Reason.

Learn the moral impotence of time to blot out sin. There is a moral memory. Conscience never forgets, although intellect does. See ch. 50:15.

24. Twenty years of harsh experience had not destroyed the tender feelings of Joseph's heart.

28. Troubled by an act of generosity and consideration! By the mercies of God!

36. Think of a man writing a history of his life, and God writing it in a parallel column!

43 : 23. Preaching peace in his Master's name.

45 : 9. Contrast the story of Joseph's career with the story of the prodigal son. God does not wait to call us unto him till we become lords.

27. Jacob always had an eye for the practical, and when he saw the waggons his heart revived. Christ had to become man before he could teach us.

46 : 34. We are the sheep; Christ the shepherd; and both are abominable to the world.

48 : 3. Where will Jacob begin in his autobiography? Not at his early scheming and deception, but at his second birth. Not at his fleshly birthday which was in reality his death-day. Ps. 79: 8.

19. What memories Jacob must have had when he gave the blessing to Joseph's younger son!

49 : 22. Ths boys outside got some of the fruit. If we are overflowing, the world around will get some of the benefit.

EXODUS.

Genesis left Israel in Egypt as a "house," or family. See Gen. 50: 22.

Exodus leaves them a nation of about two million souls (ch. 18: 21–24), with chiefs, code of laws, judicature, and settled form of worship.

Exodus finds them a "family" (ch. 1: 1–6), and leaves them a theocracy, the people of God. Ch. 30: 3–13; 29: 6, 40: 34. See John 3: 16.

1 : 9. All bad kings have feared the rise of manhood. Never neglect young life.

10. In dealing with the children of Israel, nothing better than murder occurred to this short-sighted king. He never thought of culture, kindness, social development, etc.

2 : 1. Renown may have obscurity for a pedestal.

2: 3. Jochebed laid the ark in the flags by the river's brink, but first she laid it on the heart of God.

8. Where the heart is moved to do some noble and heroic thing, the first thought should be taken as an inspiration from God. Do n't think about it, but do it.

We call the early life of Moses miraculous, and find in our own nothing to excite religious wonder or thankfulness.

12. Rashness makes work for repentance. Judges 11 : 31; Dan. 6 : 14. Moses killed the Egyptian and next day his influence was gone. Murder for liberty; wrong committed for the right.

14. So Christ was rejected by his brethren. Matt. 10 : 36.

17. Men can be held by the heart forever, but not by the throat.

3 : Objections raised by Moses for declining and avoiding God's call: —
Lack of fitness. V. 11.
" " words. V. 13.
" " authority. Chap. 4 : 1.
" " powers of speech. 4 : 10.
" " special adaptation. 4 : 13.
" " success at first attempt. 5 : 23.
" " acceptance by Israelites. 6 : 12.

1. Moses had gone back to the occupation of his ancestors.

5. Under the law: "Put off thy shoes."

Under grace: "Put shoes on his feet." Luke 15 : 22.

3 : 10. The call of Moses.

11. "Who am I?" God could have accomplished the exodus by an angel, or by a word, but he uses men to speak to men. Mediators. See 1 Tim. 2 : 5.

14. Whose business was Moses going on? Magnify your office. Do not belittle your duty.

Moses remembered his failure, in chap. 2.

"I AM that I AM." "A name as mysteriously human as the bush is mysteriously equal to the solemn occasion: another name not human at all in its first impression on the mind, a verb whose conjugation cannot go beyond the first line, an 'I AM' that doubles back upon itself, and waits with mysterious patience 'to become flesh and dwell among us.'"

God did not date far back into history, but placed himself in living relations with men with whom Moses was familiar. See v. 6.

4 : 1. We are not told to be successful, but to be obedient. It is the work of the Spirit to make men believe; we must deliver the message. Every preacher has to face human mistrust.

5. When God joined himself to Moses's rod, it worked wonders.

10. Moses's excuse now becomes personal. He claims

he is not eloquent, yet, in Deut. 32 : 1, he calls heavens and earth to hear him.

As if the Maker of man's mouth could not touch his lips with eloquence !

Not eloquence, but truth. 1 Cor. 2 : 1–5. — Paul.

Don't be self-conscious. Think of Moses turning his great mission into a question of his own eloquence !

4 : 13. What Moses would have missed if God had chosen Aaron, or Joshua, or Caleb instead ! John 6 : 66.

21. Hardening of Pharaoh's heart. See chapter 7 : 13. If a man rejects mercy he becomes hardened. The same sun that melts the ice hardens the clay. See Ps. 81 : 12 ; 2 Thess. 2 : 11 ; Gen. 6 : 3.

If you want to see what hardening would do, look at Pharaoh ; if you want to see what mercy would do, look at Israel. Both failed.

A child can treat God with sulkiness and silence. The tiniest knee can stiffen and refuse to bow before him.

Without water, clay becomes like stone. Without the grace of God, the heart becomes hard.

24. Moses had married into the world, and now his reaping-time had come.

We may learn three things from the plagues : —
1. The divine right in life.
2. Human opposition to divine voices.
3. God always wins. Acts 9 : 5 ; Ps. 99 : 1.

7 : 19. The first plague was to turn the waters of Egypt into blood. The first miracle of Jesus was to turn water into wine (joy). See John 2 : 1-12.

We wonder about the river turned into blood, but not about the heart turned into stone.

8 : 15. "When Pharaoh saw there was respite, he hardened his heart, and hearkened not unto" Moses and Aaron. Like the newsboy who only said his prayers at night; he could take care of himself by day.

9 : 11. The power of the magicians broke down at last. You cannot run the whole race with God : He will conquer in the end.

27. Pharaoh's first confession of sin.

12 : Redemption.

There must have been at least two hundred and fifty thousand lambs slain at Passover ; yet we never find the word "lambs." "Kill *it*" — one grand representation of the Lamb of God.

6. Not a live lamb. Not the life of Christ, but his death and his blood are efficacious.

7, 8. The blood of the lamb was safety.

The flesh of the lamb was nourishment.

33. Pharaoh at first said the children of Israel should not go out of Egypt, but God said they should. Unbelief says, "No." Fear says, "No." The devil says, "No." But God says, "Yes."

13 : Sanctification.

The Passover shows the work of Christ, whose blood cleanses from sin.

The Red Sea passage — his work in delivering his people from the power of Satan.

The passage of Jordan — our standing in Christ's resurrection.

13 : 21. While you are in the wilderness, the only way to walk is to follow the cloud of glory.

14 : Deliverance.

10. Old enemies pursuing. You don't step right out of Egypt on to the throne of God. Old sins and habits assert themselves. The devil never says "Good-bye." After you think he is dead, he turns up in your heart.

13. Moses said, "Stand still." The Lord said, "Go forward": which was their salvation.

No one can "go forward" in the strength of God, until he has first "stood still" in his own helplessness.

20. "The one came not near the other all the night." It must amaze the devil, says John Mc Neill, that he has not gotten us before now. When everything seems in his favor, and we seem to be selling ourselves to him, there is an invisible and impenetrable wall between us, and he has not gotten us yet.

22. Faith *seems* to be as feeble as a wall of waters : but it is strong as a wall of iron.

25 : Triumph.

1. The redeemed sing this same song in heaven. Rev. 15 : 3.

There was no song in Egypt. Infidelity has no songs.

15:13. "Led forth," then "guided."

23. Bitter waters after the passage of the Red Sea. Life's greatest triumphs may be succeeded by vexatious incidents, even though you *are* in the right path.

16:21. The daybreak blessing is a day-long gain.
Seek the heavenly manna in the morning of your life.

32. The way to enrich life is to keep a retentive memory in the heart.

17:9. First mention of Joshua. He was probably forty-five years old.

18:25. "Moses chose able men out of all Israel and made them heads over all the people." Moses never thought that hitherto he had been letting the talents of others lie idle.

19:5. "Ye shall be a peculiar treasure unto me above all people." The gospel originated in heaven; no desire was first expressed by the people.
God first prepares the heart, later he gives the word of the law.

8. "All that the Lord hath spoken we will do." Bold and self-confident language. The golden calf, the broken tables, the neglected ordinances, the stoned messengers, the rejected and crucified

Christ, are overwhelming evidence of man's dishonored vows.

20 : If man puts himself under the law, it is duty or damnation.
The ten commandments exhibit : —
1. God's strict justice.
2. Man's awful depravity.

8–11. Under the law, they labored first, then rested. But under grace we first find rest in Jesus, and then work.

25. No hewn stone — "no works," no human effort. "If thou lift up thy tool upon it, thou hast polluted it."— *Polluted*, not polished.

26. We have no steps to climb when we approach God.

24 : The Old Testament Transfiguration.
Under the law :
V. 1. "Afar off."
V. 2. "Not come nigh," "neither go up."
Under grace :
Heb. 4 : 16. "Come boldly unto the throne of grace."
Heb. 10 : 22. "Let us draw near."
We may search from end to end of the legal ritual, and not find the words "draw nigh."

25 : The inspired house, like the inspired Book, employs only willing hands to carry out God's plans. Invention is not invited.

18. The cherubim represent "the redeemed." Ezekiel's living creatures were cherubim (Eze. 10 : 20), and in Rev. 5 : 9 they sang, "Thou hast redeemed us."

26 : 14. The rams' skins would always remind them of the ram caught in the thicket. Gen. 22 : 13.

15. The boards, taken from nature and covered with gold, were fit for God's house. So sinners are prepared for Christ's spiritual temple.

19. The silver sockets on which the boards rested, were made out of the ransom-money. Ex. 30 : 12–16. Christians stand on the redemption of Christ.

28 : 12. Aaron bore the names of the twelve tribes on his shoulders. So Christ bears the church. Luke 15 : 5.

29 : 4. "Wash." A clean body for a clean soul.

10. Identification with the offering : hence death, v. 11; atonement, v. 12; judgment satisfied in God's acceptance, vs. 13, 14.

20. The ear — God-ward — hear.
hand — man-ward — work.
foot — earth-ward — walk.
The same rites were used in consecrating the priest and in cleansing the leper !

33. "But a stranger shall not eat thereof, because they are holy." No more should an unconverted man partake of the Lord's Supper.

39. "The one lamb thou shalt offer in the morning;

and the other lamb thou shalt offer at even." This custom was kept up for fifteen hundred years.

30 : 15. One ransom-price for all. So one Christ for all. Both within reach of rich and poor, who are on a level as regards redemption.

31 : 2. Bezaleel = in the shadow of God.
Uri = light of Jehovah.
For the work of the tabernacle, or of the ministry, there should be : —
  (1.) The divine selection and call.
    V. 2. "I have called."
    V. 6. "I have given."
        John 3 : 27.
  (2.) The divine qualification.
    V. 3. "I have filled."
    V. 6. "I have put wisdom."
  (3.) The divine commandment.
    V. 6. "I have commanded."

32 : 1. "How singularly like the apostasy of professing Christendom in the last days, as foretold by Christ and his apostles, is this apostasy of Israel. They were tested by the prolonged absence of Moses, as the Church is tested by the prolonged absence of Christ. In Matt. 24 : 48, our Saviour teaches us that the apostasy begins by the evil servant saying, 'My Lord delayeth his coming.' In Matt. 25 : 19, we read, 'After a long time the Lord of those servants cometh and reckoneth with them.' In 2 Peter 3 : 3, 4, we read, 'There shall come in the last days scoffers, walking after their own lusts and saying, Where is the promise of his coming?' Human nature is the same from generation to generation."

When Moses was gone, Aaron failed. He was not God-called and chosen.

"Up, make us gods." Manufactured gods! The graving tool of unbelief (v. 4).

11-13. Moses found no plea in Israel's conduct or character, but only in the glory of God, the vindication of his holy name, and the accomplishment of his oath.

14. God's repenting is not a change of his will but of his work.

28. Three thousand lose their life at the proclamation of the law. Three thousand gained life everlasting at the first preaching of the gospel.

33. Under the law God speaks of blotting out the *sinner;* under grace, he is seen blotting out *sin.*

33:18. When Moses met God at the burning bush, he was afraid; but when he got better acquainted, he was bold.

34:6,7. Note the attributes of God:—

Merciful; gracious; longsuffering; abundant in goodness, and truth; keeping mercy for thousands; forgiving iniquity and transgression and sin; by no means clearing the guilty; visiting the iniquity of the fathers upon the children.

29. "Moses wist not that the skin of his face shone." Spurgeon said of a certain man that he always thought he was sinless until the man said so himself!

The Athenians at one time used to have their prisoners tried in the dark, lest their countenances should influence the judges.

The face is often a better witness than the lips.

35: In this chapter we have: —

Willing hearts — three times, vs. 5, 22, 29.
Wise hearts — three times, vs. 10, 25, 35.
Heart stirred — twice, vs. 21, 26.
Heart to teach — once, v. 34.

Free will in the work, vs. 5, 21, 22, 29.
Fitted for the work, vs. 10, 25, 31, 34, 35.
Fired to the work, vs. 21, 26.

4–10. Note the qualifications here given for partnership in the Lord's work: —
1. Out of Egypt: redeemed by blood.
2. Commanded by God to do the thing.
3. Willing-hearted to give.
4. Wise-hearted to make.
5. Eager-hearted to act.

Men would murmur less if they worked more.

36 : 6. "And Moses gave commandment, and they caused it to be proclaimed throughout the camp, saying, Let neither man nor woman make any more work for the offering of the sanctuary." Many would be late. How they would be filled with remorse!

38 : 8. The laver of brass not only furnished water for the priests to wash in, but its shining, polished surface revealed any spots or pollution in them.

LEVITICUS.

The Offerings.

1 : 3. What shall I bring? Myself. Romans 12 : 1. "I beseech you therefore, brethren, by the mercies of God, that ye present your bodies a living sacrifice, holy, acceptable unto God: which is your reasonable service."
Whereto? the cross.
How? Willingly. In spirit and in truth. John 4: 23.

4. "He shall put his hand upon the head of the burnt-offering." This implies confession, substitution, atonement, satisfaction, forgiveness.

9. The careful cleansing of the sacrifice before it was placed on the altar, teaches of God's holiness and the righteous requirements of His law. What God accepts must be clean.

8 : 4. It is said fifty times of Moses that he "did as the Lord commanded him."

9 : 3, 4. Sin-offering: Christ the sin-bearer.
Burnt-offering: Consecration. Rom. 12: 1.
Peace-offering: Christ our peace. Eph. 2: 14–16.
Meat-offering: Feeding on the Word.

6. "The glory of the Lord *shall appear* unto you."

23. "The glory of the Lord *appeared* unto all the people."

11 : 3. Parting the hoof — outward walk.
Chewing the cud — inward life.

35. Precaution against sin and defilement, in the kitchen as well as in the tabernacle.

14 : V. 5. One bird killed — Christ dying on the cross.
V. 7. One bird loosed — Christ risen and ascended on high.

15 : 10. Influence over others.

19 : 27. Baal-worshipers rounded their beard and hair to make their faces look like the sun. Avoid the appearance of evil.

23 : Seven feasts : —
1. Sabbath — Rest.
2. Passover — Death of Christ.
3. First-fruits — Resurrection.
4. Pentecost — Descent of the Holy Spirit.
5. Trumpets — Ingathering of Israel.
6. Atonement — Mourning for sin.
7. Tabernacles — Christ's indwelling in the Christian.

25 : 5. The only place in the Bible where the word "its" occurs.

10. "Liberty throughout all the land unto all the inhabitants thereof." Inscribed on the Independence Bell that rang in Philadelphia, July 4, 1776.

NUMBERS.

1 : 18. The Christian's pedigree.
"Sons of God." 1 John 3 : 2.
"Children of God by faith in Jesus Christ." Gal. 3 : 26.
"Heirs of God." Gal. 3 : 29 ; Rom. 8 : 14, 17.

6 : 12. Lost days !

24–26. Here is a benediction that can go all the world over, and can give all the time without being impoverished. Every heart may utter it : it is the speech of God : every letter may conclude with it ; every day may begin with it ; every night may be sanctified by it. Here is blessing — keeping — shining — the uplifting upon our poor life of all heaven's glad morning. It is the Lord himself who brings this bar of music from heaven's infinite anthems.

27. All differences disappear — all tribal names pass out of view ; and the name of Jehovah is upon all.

11 : 31. "Upon" should be "above." Gen. 1 : 2, 20; 8 : 1; Zech. 5 : 3.

12 : 1. The Jew has ever been jealous of the Gentile being received into the covenant. Eph. 3 : 6.

15. The sin of God's people still hinders the progress of his cause.

13 : Faith says, "We are well able." V. 30.
Unbelief says, "We are not able." V. 31.

13 : 31. Israel said, "We be not able." But the weakness of God is stronger than men. 1 Cor. 1 : 25.

32. Israel said, "The land eateth up the inhabitants." God's word was, "They are bread for us." Chapter 14 : 9.

33. Israel said, "We are grasshoppers in their sight." God said, those nations were "as a drop of a bucket:" "as the small dust of the balance:" "as grasshoppers." Isa. 40 : 15, 22.

14 : 16. Our unsuccess attributed to God.

33. "Your children shall wander in the wilderness forty years." So Christians wander about, and call it Christian progress !

Many die in the wilderness; their souls are saved, but their lives are lost.

18 : 19. "A covenant of salt" — a perpetuity of God's covenant mercies.

21 : 6. The Hebrew for "fiery serpents" is "seraphim," for their burning heat and glow. See Luke 10 : 18, where Satan is called a fallen seraph.

21 : 7. God does not always answer in the letter, but in the spirit, of prayer. He did not remove the fiery serpents, but provided a remedy. We live among serpents still, and must look to Christ for salvation.

There was no particular "reason" in the brazen serpent; but *God* was in it.

22 : 23. The ass saw the angel which Balaam saw not.

His eyes were blinded by the dust of covetousness.

23 : 10. "Let me die the death of the righteous, and let my last days be like his." Why not rather live the life of the righteous?

You cannot live a vicious life and die a righteous death.

19. There are three things God cannot do : —
1. He cannot lie.
2. He cannot deny himself.
3. He cannot see our sins through the blood of Jesus Christ.

God writes with a pen that never blots, and speaks with a tongue that never slips, and acts with a hand that never fails.

26 : 51. 601,730 as against 603,550 in chapter 1. Israel's growth ceased for forty years. So it may be with us as churches, and so forth, if we are unbelieving.

27 : 1. The first movement for women's rights.

12. Moses (representing the Law) was not to have the privilege of leading the Israelites into the promised land. It was for Joshua (Jesus) to do so.

13. Old age is a sunset and a sunrise in one. We cannot climb the hills as in youth, but we can mount up as on eagle's wings, if we have found in Christ the secret of eternal life.

28 : Offerings and sacrifices.

   3. Daily.

   9. Weekly.

  11. Monthly.

32 : 23. You cannot bury your sins so deep but they will have a resurrection by and by, unless they have been washed away by the blood of Christ.

DEUTERONOMY.

1 : 44. "Chased you as bees do, and destroyed you." "The sting of death is sin."

2 : 31. The Lord does not give all at once. It is according to our readiness to take that he gives. Chap. 3 : 24.

3 : 23. Moses, Elijah (1 Kings 19 : 4), and Paul (2 Cor. 12 : 8) all prayed; but God answered in his own way.

6 : 6. Consecration in the heart first.

  12. Full flesh often causes heart failure. So prosperity often proves a danger to piety.

16 : The holy feasts were (in general) appointed for these ends and uses : —

    1. To distinguish the people of God from other nations.

    2. To keep afoot the remembrance of the benefits already received.

    3. To be a type and figure of benefits yet

further to be conferred upon them by Christ.
4. To unite God's people in holy worship.
5. To preserve purity in holy worship prescribed by God.

The Passover, Pentecost, and Feast of Tabernacles typify a completed redemption:—
1. By the passion of the cross : Suffering.
2. By the coming of the Holy Spirit : Grace.
3. By the final triumph of the coming King : Glory.

21 : 22. "And if a man have committed a sin worthy of death, . . . and thou hang him on a tree, his body shall not remain all night upon the tree."

Only two instances of the observance of this law fully recorded: Joshua 8 : 29 — the wicked king of Ai; and John 19 : 31 — the King of Glory.

28 : 25. "Thou shalt be removed into all the kingdoms of the earth." Over the entrance to a cemetery in New Orleans are these words (in Hebrew): "The dispersed of Judah."

28 : 32. "Thy sons and thy daughters shall be given unto another people." In the horrible persecutions of the Jews by the Romanists in Spain, four centuries ago, their children were stripped from them to be reared in the Popish faith.

33. "The fruit of thy land and all thy labors shall a nation which thou knowest not, eat up : and

> thou shalt be only oppressed and crushed alway." Fulfilled under the Assyrians, and Romans, for centuries, and now fulfilled under the Turks, who, by their misrule, do literally "eat up" the lands they govern.

58, 59. During the scourging of Jewish culprits these two verses used to be read, and, immediately after them, Psalms 78 and 38.

65, 66. The case of every backslider: "Thou shalt find no ease, neither shall the sole of thy foot have rest: but the Lord shall give thee there a trembling heart, and failing of eyes, and sorrow of mind."

29 : 5. When the Lord leads, he provides shoe-leather.

19. There is not one of the Christian graces and fruits that the devil does not counterfeit.

19–21. The Lord is absolute in threatening and resolute in punishing.

32 : 10. Precept: "Keep my law as the apple of thine eye." Prov. 7 : 2.
Prayer: "Keep me as the apple of thine eye." Ps. 17 : 8.

33 :   V. 3. "Hand,"— Safety.
"Feet,"— Learning.
V. 12. "Side,"— Fellowship.
"Shoulders,"— Power.
V. 27. "Arms,"— Rest.
29. Saved — shielded — defended.

"Thine enemies shall be found liars unto thee," i. e., thy character shall be restored.

34 : 4. "This is the land which I sware unto Abraham. . . . I have caused thee to see it with thine eyes, but thou shalt not go over thither."

This was Moses's second great disappointment. At the age of forty, he thought the Israelites would choose him as their leader.

JOSHUA.

Miriam, Aaron, and Moses, all died before the passage of the Jordan. Prophet, Priest, and Law bring us to the borders of the promised land. Only Jesus, our Joshua, can lead us into our inheritance.

The rod was Moses's symbol.

The spear was Joshua's symbol.

1 : 8. God's instructions for Bible study.

7 : 1. Only one Achan in the camp: but Israel was defeated on his account.

10. Prayer before repentance is unavailing. We must put away our sin.

21. Steps in Achan's sin: —
  1. "I saw."
  2. "I coveted."
  3. "I took."
  4. "I hid."

Compare Eve, Gen 3:6; Ananias, Acts 5: 1–10.

"How mean was the sin of Achan! He saw the

Babylonish garment, and all the soldier in him withered up and he became a sneaking thief."

9 : 14. "And asked not council at the mouth of the Lord." The cause of most of our wrong-doing. Eph. 6 : 18.

13 : 22. We thought we had done with Balaam, but who knows where his own name may come up again?
The mention of some brings thoughts of pain and woe; of others, joy.

33. Self-denial is best for one's self, for then we oblige God to take care of us.
He only is a happy man whose sole dependence is on God.

15 : 15. Kirjath-sepher — book-city. Dr. Gregg, of Brooklyn, says it was so called because it was the seat of a public library. Prof. Sayce says knowledge was far advanced in this early period, so that philosophy and science were common.

20 : What storms have to beat upon us before we will fall in with God's appointment and fly to Christ as our refuge.
The cities of refuge are a type of Christ, and their names are significant in that connection. Kadesh means holy, and our refuge is in the holy Jesus; Shechem, a shoulder, "and the government is upon his shoulder;" Hebron, fellowship, and believers are called into the fellowship of Christ Jesus our Lord; Bezer, a fortification, for He is a stronghold to all them that trust in Him;

Rainoth, high, or exalted, "for him hath God exalted with his own right hand;" Golan, joy, or exultation, for in Him all the saints are justified and shall glory.

As the cities of refuge were so situated as to be accessible from every part of the land, so Christ is ever accessible to needy sinners. 1 John 2:1, 2.

22:26. An altar of witness, that was not commanded. The motive was good, but it may have led their children astray. Cf. Ornate altars, etc., in churches.

23:6. Courage in obedience!

14. Joshua had tried God forty years in the brickkilns, forty years in the desert, and thirty years in the promised land, and this was his dying testimony.

JUDGES.

Weak things made strong.
    The left hand. Chap. 3:21.
    An ox-goad. 3:31.
    A woman. 4:14.
    A nail. 4:21.
    A barley-cake. 7:13.
    Pitcher and trumpet. 7:20.
    Piece of millstone. 9:53.
    Jaw-bone of an ass. 15:16.

3, 4, 5: Note the steps in Israel's trouble. They —
    1. Failed to drive out the idolaters.

       2. Dwelt among them.
       3. Inter-married with them.
       4. Served their gods.
       5. Forgot God, and
       6. Were sold by God to their enemies.

5 : 23. The sin of omission. Do-Nothing's curse:—
"Curse ye Meroz, curse ye bitterly the inhabitants thereof, because they came not to the help of the Lord."

    24. "Blessed *above* women shall Jael be." She got a higher salutation than the virgin— "Blessed art thou *among* women." Luke 1 : 28, 42.

6 : 15. Gideon's power came through humiliation.

7 : 16. Empty pitchers — light shining in them — trumpets to proclaim. Such should Christians be.

15 : 5. The country was undivided by hedge or fence, so that once a fire started, it would burn the whole crop.

16 : 4. Samson was at a bad place, for a bad purpose, and of course he came to a bad end.

    19. Sleeping in the lap of temptation.

17 : 6. Every man did that which was right in his own eyes, and then they soon did that which was evil in the sight of God.
This verse is the key to the book. It is the teaching of the socialist and anarchist; but it did not work in Israel.

RUTH.

Subject, the redeemer.
Chapter 1. Decision.
" 2. Toil.
" 3. Rest.
" 4. Reward.

Ruth is the one book of the Old Testament that sets forth the person of the Redeemer.

1:6. The true child of God never dies in the far country, but returns to his Father's house.

7. To get to Bethlehem you must leave Moab.

14. Orpah — profession : Ruth — possession.

21. "I went out."
"The Lord hath brought me home."
Boaz — a type of Christ : —
Lord of the harvest.
Near kinsman.
Supplier of wants.
Redeemer of the inheritance.
Man who gives rest.
Wealthy kinsman.
Bridegroom.

I SAMUEL.

2:1. The heart is at rest after answered prayer.

4:18. Old Eli's heart (by reason of his sons' conduct and the disaster they brought on the ark of God) was broken before his neck.

5 : 4. There is a tradition that when Christ was brought into Egypt, all the idols fell. When Christ enters the heart, all idols fall before him.

7 : 7. The Israelites had learned one useful lesson — to be afraid of the Philistines. So the church and the world.

9 : 2. Believers are among others what Saul was among the Israelites, the tallest by head and shoulders.

3. Saul went out after asses and found a nation of them ready to make him king.

10 : 6. "Another man."

9. "Another heart."

11 : 2. When man makes a covenant with sin, he must pay dearly for his pleasure.

12 : 7. "Stand and listen."

16. "Stand and see."

20. Satan tempts man to presume, then to despair.

24, 25. How to serve the Lord.
Why serve the Lord.
Results of not serving Him.

15 : 22. Sacrifice without obedience is sacrilege.

24. Saul feared the people and became cowardly and disobedient. A man who fears God need have no other fear.

30. Saul said, "I have sinned." David said, "I have sinned *against the Lord*." 2 Sam. 12 : 13.

David said, "Create in me a clean heart." Ps. 51 : 10. Saul says, "Don't let the people know my heart is not clean."

There is little worth in outward splendor, if virtue yield it not an inward luster.

16 : 13. In 1065 B. C. no one took David as king.
Three years later he had 400 followers. 1 Sam. 22 : 2.
Four years later he had 600 followers. 1 Sam. 27 : 2.
A great host. 1 Chron. 12 : 22.
Three years later, "The men of Judah." 2 Sam. 2 : 4.
The men of Israel. 2 Sam. 2 : 17 ; 5 : 3.
See the accessions to the disciples, in Acts.

18. David's "comely" person ; his pastime ; his patriotism ; his prudence ; his piety ; the Lord was with him.

17 : 8. No preacher can build up his church without the active co-operation of the members. He is not a Goliath to go forth alone, but a leader, under God, to direct others.

37. There were doubtless many in Saul's army who knew God *could* use them to overcome Goliath, but David was the only one who knew God *would* use him.

The atheist counts his enemies; the saint looks up to God.

18:1,2. Saul took David to his home, but Jonathan took him to his heart.

20 : 3. "There is but a step between me and death." The "step" was forty-seven years. Under God's care, it was a long one.

21 : 8. The King's business must be done —
 a. With haste.
 b. Heartily. Col. 3 : 23.
 c. Diligently. Ezra 7 : 23.

22 : 2. **D**ISTRESS.
 EBT.
 ISCONTENT.

30 : 13. Two good questions: —
 To whom belongest thou?
 Whence art thou?

II SAMUEL.

1 : 10. Saul neglected to punish Agag the Amalekite, and at his death he was stripped of his crown and ornaments by a prowling Amalekite.

3 : 3. David married a princess who was not of Israel, in order to strengthen his kingdom: and Absalom was her son.

11 : 2. Absalom was guilty of incest at the same place as David his father — on the king's roof.
 Chap. 16 : 2. As you sow, you will reap.

8. Do you stumble at the lives of some of these Bible characters? The Bible tells how salvation comes to the sinner, not to the righteous. Chap. 12 : 14.

12 : 1. A short sermon from a God-sent man.

When his hearers resented St. Augustine's frequent reproofs, he said: "Change your conduct and I will change my conversation."

The rough hewing of reproof is only to square us for the heavenly building.

7. Notice the "I's," "thou's," "thee's." A pointed and personal application.

14. "By this deed thou hast given great occasion to the enemies of the Lord to blaspheme." How often David is held up by infidels now! The Scripture is fulfilled.

A man may become of no use in this universe except as a warning—"to point a moral, or adorn a tale."

If you commit one sin, it will cause you many sorrows and the world many triumphs.

The world will sooner make an excuse for its own enormities than for your infirmities.

14 : 15. Not only must we talk to Jesus, but we must listen to him. Not pray less, but listen more.

18 : 18. Cato said he would rather have men ask why he had no monument, than why he had one.

19 : 2. Many can mourn over a body from which the soul has departed, when they do not mourn over a soul whom God has deserted.

22 : Praise for deliverance!

23 : 11. The patch of lentils was a small thing to fight for; but Shammah was fighting on the right side, and the Lord wrought a great victory through him.

20. "Benaiah . . . went down also and slew a lion in the midst of a pit in time of snow." So Christ left the Father and came down to earth to kill *sin* in our fallen nature.

I KINGS.

2 : 27. God never forgets. One hundred and twenty years had elapsed since the sentence on Eli's house was pronounced.

3 : 26. The devil does not mind if a man's heart is divided; but Christ, the true lover of hearts, must have it all or none.

8 : 56. Unclaimed promises are like uncashed checks. They will keep you from bankruptcy, but not from want.

10 : 8. As Solomon was magnified by the words and conduct of his servants, so Jesus ought to be honored by the words and conduct of Christians.

17 : 16. Some one has said of Christianity that the more you export, the more you have at home.

18 : 28. Trying to make a blood-covenant with Baal.

19 : 10. "I have been very jealous for the Lord God of hosts. . . . I, even I only am left." Elijah indulged in three capital "I's" here.

18. There are a great many Christians who have life, but like the seven thousand who had not bowed

I KINGS.

unto Baal, they are not good for much when it takes the Almighty to find them. See Acts 18:10.

II KINGS.

2:1-10. Testing before blessing.

1. What events Elijah and Elisha would chat about as they passed through Gilgal, Jericho, Bethel, and Jordan, recalling God's dealings with their fathers in former days! Gilgal, a new start, Josh. 5:6; Bethel, no confidence in the flesh, Gen. 28; Jericho, the manifestation of Jehovah's power in times gone by; Jordan, can the Lord's presence do the same to-day?

   Gilgal — circumcision; public profession.
   Bethel — church going.
   Jericho — Bible study (school of the prophets).
   Jordan — death to the world; consecration.

   What are any of these worth if you "tarry" while the Lord goes on? Go with him through these stages, then return to the world in his power, to glorify him, to make the bitter sweet (v. 19), etc.

11. The three dispensations had each a representative who went directly to heaven — Enoch, ante-diluvians; Elijah, children of Abraham; Christ, the church.

   To-day we look upon an ascended Saviour.

14. Faith before knowledge.

4:21. The Shunamite woman laid her dead boy on the prophet's bed, determining to give him no rest until he restored him to life.

5 : 3. A little maid said a few words that made a commotion in two kingdoms. God honored her faith by doing for Naaman, the idolater, what he had not done for any in Israel. See Luke 4 : 27.

How often has the finger of childhood pointed grown-up persons in the right direction.

The maid boasted of God that he would do for Naaman what he had not done for any in Israel; and God honored her faith.

5 : 10. Naaman had two diseases — pride and leprosy. The first needed curing as much as the second.

14. Naaman had (1) to get down from his chariot of pride ; (2) afterwards, to wash according to the prescribed way.

6 : 14. Trying to catch God! Herod tried it (Matt. 2 : 16), and the Jews, when they killed Jesus. The hosts of hell now encompass Christians in our cities.

16. Two classes only, "with" or "against" us (Matt. 24 : 34, 41).

17. The horses and chariots were not made for the occasion ; they were all there, and only the eye failed. The eye of faith could see them.

7 : 2. "If you would believe, you must crucify the question, 'how?'" See Mark 8 : 4.

8 : 13. We do not know ourselves.

10 : 31. "Departed not"— better, "renounced not," did not take active part against.

I CHRONICLES.

15 : 16. Sacred music, vocal and instrumental.

29 : 5. Co-workers with King David.

    11. Do not sing or preach to your own praise. "*Thine*, O Lord, is the greatness."

    17. A tried heart, an upright heart.

    18. A thankful heart, a prepared heart.

    19. A perfect heart.

II CHRONICLES.

7 : 14. The pathway of blessing : "If my people, which are called by my name, shall humble themselves, and pray, and seek my face, and turn from their wicked ways : then will I hear from heaven, and will forgive their sin, and will heal their land."
It brings heaven within speaking-distance.

12 : 14. "Prepared"—margin, "fixed." There is no fixity of purpose in the sinner.

14 : 11. Dependence upon God.
Confession of weakness.
Confidence in His help.
Request.

    12. Request granted.

18 : 11. Ahab had his preachers and prophets. No man is so corrupt, but he will find some one who preaches to suit him.

30. Do not try to overcome your failings and mistakes one by one ; but deal at once with the cause of your failure.

20 : 21, 22. Praise first, then victory.

35. Man never gains by doing wrong in order that good may come of it.

EZRA.

3 : 8. First the temple is built ; afterward, (in Nehemiah) the walls of the city — the inner before the outer. Cleanse the heart and all else will be clean.

7 : 10. Ezra prepared his heart, not his head, to seek the law of the Lord, and to do it.

NEHEMIAH.

Nehemiah had seven forms of opposition in his work : —

1. The laughter of the enemy, chapter 2 : 19.
2. " grief " " " " 2 : 10.
3. " wrath " " " " 4 : 1.
4. " mocking " " " " 4 : 3.
5. " conflict with " " " 4 : 8.
6. " subtility of " " " 6 : 1.
   By " within, " 6 : 10.
7. " craft without " 11 : 35.

Nehemiah began his work in prayer. Chap. 1 : 4, "I prayed before the God of heaven."

Nehemiah continued his work in prayer. Chap. 4 : 4. "Hear, O our God."

Nehemiah did not cease at the end of his work. Chap. 8:31, "Remember me, O my God, for good."

3:10. "Against his house." There is work for Christ at home, as well as in foreign lands.

4: 8. Hindrances:—
What things are hindrances?
How can they be removed?

13. Walk, war, and work.

8: The word "understand" occurs six times in this chapter, vs. 2, 3, 7, 8, 12, 13.

13:18. A warning from history.

24. They intermarried with the heathen; hence, mixed principles and mixed speech.

ESTHER.

The name of God is not found in Esther, but the activity of God is — overruling history, rewarding the good, punishing the evil, etc. It is the one book in the Bible devoted to showing the providence of God in human affairs.

This book teaches:—
1. The overruling providence of God.
2. His love for his own people.
3. His power to overturn the devices of the wicked.

JOB.

Job has no mention of the ancient patriarchs or old Jews.

1 : 1. Job is called "perfect" here: in last chapter, verse 6, he "abhors himself." The more one grows in grace, the meaner he is in his own eyes.

8. "There is none like him in all the earth." Job was so like God that there was none like him.

12. Men and devils can only give what God prescribes: they cannot themselves appoint our physic.

21. Affliction is like the wind that blows one vessel into port, another to destruction.

"How much did he leave?" said a man when the death of a wealthy friend was mentioned. "*He left it all.*"

2 : 3. Job was a perfect man, but needing correction.

3 : 3. Instead of cursing the sin in which he was born, Job cursed the day in which he was born.

5 : 17. By chastening, the Lord separates the sin that he hates, from the sinner whom he loves.

7 : 13. God sometimes puts his children to bed in the dark.

14 : 14. "If a man die, shall he live again?" Answered by Christ at Lazarus's grave. They looked for resurrection before Christ's time. See Acts 23: 6; 24:14, 15; 2 Sam. 12:23; Acts 26:6, 7; 28:20.

18 : 14. Death may be the king of terrors, but Jesus is King of kings.

19 : 25, 26. Redemption — Resurrection.

23 : 10. God's furnaces are still burning: e. g., physical suffering, mental distress. Gold comes forth pure, precious. Cf. Mal. 3:3.

29 : Job says "I," twenty times. Cf. Chap. 42:6.

Some men write the letter small — "i" — but no one can get rid altogether of the self-life. One cannot jump from his shadow; but if he turns toward the sun, it is cast behind; and if he stands beneath it at its zenith his shadow is beneath his feet.

33 : 4. "The spirit of God hath made me, and the breath of the Almighty hath given me life." You have but one arrow to shoot at the mark. If it be shot at random, God may never put another into your bow.

V. 24. Ruin, Ransom.

V. 25. Regeneration.

V. 26. Reconciliation, Righteousness.

V. 28. Resurrection.

34 : 21-24. Hiding from the presence of God. See Gen. 3:8, 10; Matt. 10:26.

Hiding under false hopes. See Ps. 10:11; Job 8:13, 16.

Hiding under false peace. 1 Thess. 5:3; Matt. 25:44, 46.

Hiding under self-righteousness. Luke 18:11, 12; Rom. 10:1-4; Job 29.

Hiding under God's works. Acts 8:9-13.

Hiding under a lie. Acts 5:1-11; 2 Kings 5:25; Isa. 28:17.

Hiding desired at judgment time. Rev. 6:12-17.

23. A boy received a number of parcels from his father, to carry. His brother said, "You have got too many." "Never mind," he replied, "father knows how many I can carry."

38 : 7. "The morning stars sang together"—vibrated. Light is produced by motion.

42 : 2. The Lord's doing and thoughts.— Margin.

  6. "I abhor myself, and repent in dust and ashes."
Moses hid his face at the burning bush. Ex. 3: 6.
Peter realized his sinfulness. Luke 5: 8.
Paul fell to the earth. Acts 9: 4.
John "fell at His feet as dead." Rev. 1: 17.

 13. God doubled Job's family. He had ten children on earth and ten in heaven.

 14. Jemima — dove.
Kezia — cassia.
Keren-happuch — horn of paint.
Three names signifying beauty; so that Job's leprosy left no taint.

PSALMS.

In Job man had been taught to know himself. In Psalms he is taught to know the Lord.

1 : 1. Walketh, standeth, sitteth.

 3. All the Lord's trees are evergreens.

3 :   T{RIAL. Vs. 1, 2.
    RUST. Vs. 3, 7.
    RIUMPH. V. 8.

4 : How to win the ungodly to Christ: —
  V. 1. Prayer for help.
  V. 2. Expostulation.
  V. 3. Warning.
  Vs. 4, 5. Exhortation.
  Vs. 6–8. Testimony to the joy of religion.

  7. The believer's heart is God's storehouse.

5 : 3. To be miserable, look within.
  To be distracted, look around.
  To be happy, look up.

8 : 4. "What are men that *He* should heed us?" cried the king of sacred song;
  "Insects of an hour, that hourly work their brother insect wrong."

9 : 8. When Roland Hill was asked what would become of the heathen, he said that if he did not meet some of them in heaven, he would see the reason why.
  V. 17. The forgotten God.
  V. 18. The unforgetting God.

11 : 5. God tests the righteous, but detests the wicked.

12 : 2. "Double heart."
  "Fixed heart." Ps. 67 : 7.
  "Glad heart." Ps. 16 : 9.

14 : 1. "The fool hath said in his heart, There is no God." The Bible was not written for fools : a wise man knows there is a God, so he need not be told so in the Bible.
  Root — no God.

Trunk — corrupt.
Fruit — abominable works.

15 : 3. Righteousness in word, act, and thought.

16 : 11. Joy: Quantity — fulness.
Dignity — at thy right hand.
Duration — forevermore.
For short sorrow, we shall have eternal joy.
For a little hunger, an eternal banquet.
For a little sickness and affliction, everlasting health and salvation.
For a little bondage, endless liberty.
For disgrace, glory.
For evil surroundings, the elect.
For Satan's temptations, the comfort of Christ.
For the lion's den, the presence of the Lion of the tribe of Judah.

17 : 15. *a.* Man's life, a sleep.
b. Death, man's awakening.
c. The inheritance at the other side.
d. Satisfaction.

19 : 7. Fourfold action of God's word : converting ; making wise ; rejoicing ; enlightening.

20 : V. 1. The defending name.
V. 5. The displayed name.
V. 7. The name depended upon.
Ps. 22. Yesterday.
Ps. 23. To-day.
Ps. 24. For ever.
Ps. 22. The good Shepherd laying down his life for his sheep.

Ps. 23. The good Shepherd blessing them.
Ps. 24. The good Shepherd leading them to the promised land.

22 : 1. This Psalm begins with the atonement-cry of Christ, and ends with the cry that indicated the finish of the atoning work.

31. The original reads : " They shall come and shall declare his righteousness unto a people that shall be born, — It is finished."

23 : "Blessed is the day," said an old divine, "when Ps. 23 was born !"

Nearly everyone can repeat Ps. 23 from memory, but not everyone from the heart.
Perfect satisfaction. V. 1.
Rest, quietness. V. 2.
Restoration, guidance. V. 3.
Consecration, joy. V. 5.
With me — the Lord.
Beneath me — green pastures.
Beside me — still waters.
Before me — a table.
Around me — mine enemies.
After me — goodness and mercy.
Ahead of me — the house of the Lord.
Happy life. V. 1.
Happy death. V. 4.
Happy eternity. V. 6.

3. "He restoreth my soul." "That's a dead 'un," said an army doctor, as he pointed to one of the bodies in the trenches before Sebastopol. "Oh, no," said the body, "I'm worth a good many dead men yet." And the "dead 'un" is now Lord Wolseley.

23 · 4. You may talk about Jesus, but as soon as you get into the valley you will talk to him.

A shadow will not hurt, but the shadow of a dog means a dog somewhere around.

5. Wherefore doth the Lord make your cup run over, but that others might taste the liquor?

6. The Shepherd leads, and goodness and mercy bring up the rear.

All God's children have two footmen, goodness and mercy, coming on behind them.

The names of God illustrated by Psalm 23.

Ps. 23 : 1. Jehovah-reah, the Lord my Shepherd.
Gen. 22 : 14. Jehovah-jireh, the Lord will provide.
Judges 6 : 24. Jehovah-shalom, the Lord send peace.
Ex. 15 : 26. Jehovah-rophi, the Lord that healeth.
Jer. 23 : 6. Jehovah-tsidkenu, the Lord our righteousness.
Eze. 48 : 35. Jehovah-shammah, the Lord is there.
Isa. 58 : 11. Jehovah-nakah, the Lord will guide thee.
Isa. 1 : 9 (Rom. 9 : 29). Jehovah-sabaoth, the Lord of hosts.
Ex. 17 : 15. Jehovah-nissi, the Lord my banner.
Jer. 51 : 56. Jehovah-gemulah, the Lord of recompense.

24 : 1. This verse is inscribed on the wall of the Royal Exchange, London.

3. "Ascend." V. 3.
"Stand in." V. 3.
"Abide." Ps. 15 : 1.

25 : 11. David prayed, "Pardon mine iniquity." Pharaoh prayed, "Take away the frogs." The latter prayed to escape the punishment; the former, the cause of it.

26 : The heart. V. 2.
Eyes. V. 3.
Hands. V. 6.
Voice. V. 7.
Feet. V. 12.

27 : 5. A man must have both feet firmly planted on the Rock before he can pull sinking men out of the floods.

28 : 1. Sometimes God is silent because of his love to us. Zeph. 3 : 17.
Sometimes, to test our faith. Matt. 15 : 23.
Sometimes, because he has spoken, but we have not listened.

30 : 5. "In His favor is life," or, "His favor is for a life-time." R. V. margin. "Life-time" contrasted with "moment." Cf. Isa. 54 : 7, 8.

32 : 1, 2. Seven steps to blessedness of forgiven sin, etc. :—
Conviction. Vs. 3, 4.
Confession. V. 5.
Forgiveness. V. 5.
Prayer. V. 6.
Protection. V. 7.

Guidance. Vs. 8, 9.
Joy. Vs. 10, 11.

1, 2. Sin forgiven and subdued.

34 : 8. Men must taste of God's grace here, or they will never taste of his glory hereafter.

36 : 1–4. Seven steps of wickedness: —
(1.) No fear of God before his eyes.
(2.) Flattereth himself in his hateful iniquity.
(3.) Words of his mouth, iniquity and deceit.
(4.) Left off to be wise and do good.
(5.) Deviseth mischief upon his bed.
(6.) Setteth himself in a way not good.
(7.) Abhorreth not evil.

37 : 38. Strauss, when dying, said to his daughter, "This is the last of me. Now we separate. I sink into nothing."

40 : 2, 3. Pit — rock — song — celebration.
Till you know the depth of the pit into which you have fallen, you will never properly praise the hand which raises you out of it.

7. "In the volume of the BOOK it is written of ME." Luther asks: "What *book* and what *person?*" "There is only one book — the Scriptures; and only one person — Jesus Christ."

41 : 4. Saul and Judas both said, "I have sinned;" David adds: "against Thee."

42 : 11. Hope is like the sun, which, as we travel toward it, casts the shadows behind us.

44 : 1. While the songs of other nations sing of the heroism of their kings, the songs of Israel celebrate the doings of God.

45 : 7. The cause,
The nature,
The measure,
>of God's anointing.

10. Four calls:—
Hearken.
Consider.
Incline thine ear.
Forget.

49 : 7, 8. The body might be redeemed from man by money (Lev. 25 : 47–49), but God himself redeems the soul. V. 15.

51 : 4. A saint says, "What have I done?" A sinner says, "What must I suffer?" One mourns for the active evil, the other for the passive evil.

52 : 5. The wicked rooted out of the land of the living.

8. The righteous rooted in the house of God.

55 : 9–11. Seven terms declaring the wickedness of the city: Violence and strife; mischief, and sorrow, and wickedness in the midst of it; deceit and guile in her streets.

19. "They have no changes, therefore they fear not God." When all goes well with a man, it is almost sure to be his ruin.

55 : 22. "Cast thy burden upon the Lord." The original is, "roll thy burden onto the Lord." We could not pick up the heavy ones and cast them.

56 : **3.** Fear should lead to faith.

11. Faith should put away fear.

58 : 2. Outward acts are more scandalous among men, but inward wickedness is more dangerous before God.

61 : Distance — the end of the earth. V. 2.
Distress — overwhelmed. V. 2.
Deliverance — the Rock. V. 2.
Defense — a shelter and a strong tower. V. 3.
Dwelling-place — thy tabernacle. V. 4.
Duration — forever. V. 7.
Destiny — abide before God. Vs. 4, 7.
Determination — I will sing praise unto thy name forever.

62 : "Only."

10. "I do not observe that grace always grows in the same ratio with a growing income."
It is often said that such a man owns millions; but most frequently the millions own the man.

63 : 1. My soul thirsteth for thee.
5. My soul shall be satisfied.
8. My soul followeth hard after thee.

7. Seven shadows:—
Wings, for shelter. Ps. 63 : 7.
Tabernacle, from daily trial. Isa. 4 : 6.

Hand, for service. Isa. 49 : 2.
Rock, for refreshment. Isa. 32 : 2.
Cloud, the Lord's presence. Isa. 4 : 5, 6.
Almighty, for power. Ps. 91 : 1.
Beloved, for rest. Cant. 2 : 3.

66 : 5. Come and see.

16. Come and hear.

66 : 12. God brings through fire and water into a wealthy place. Satan casts into fire and water in order to destroy. Mark 9 : 22.

71 : 3. Continual abiding.

14. Continual hope.

72 : 15. Continual prayer and praise.

78 : 11. A lively faith is blessed with a good memory. Forgetfulness is an early and sure sign of unbelief.

22. No sin dishonors God like unbelief.

24. Manna to eat, not to analyze.

27. Fowls for food.
Food for fowls. Ps. 79 : 2.

31. Fat in body; lean in soul. Ps. 106 : 15.

38. See note on Deut. 28 : 28.

80 : 5. "Thou feedest them with the bread of tears."
"He should have fed them also with the finest of the wheat." Ps. 81 : 16.

81 : 3. Nowadays we have made an atheist of the trumpet.

83 : 3. The Lord's "Hidden Ones":—
    With Christ in God, for salvation and life. 1 John 5 : 11, 20; Col. 3 : 3.
    Under the shadow of his wing, for shelter and safety. Ps. 17 : 8.
    In the secret of his presence, for communion with him. Ps. 31 : 20.
    In his pavilion, for testing and proving. Ps. 27 : 5; 18 : 11.
    In his quiver, ready for use. Isa. 49 : 2.
    In the shadow of his hand, for strength and service. Isa. 49 : 2.

84 : 11. The soul of man depends on God to keep it in its true orbit, just as the earth depends on the sun. Sever man from God, and he starts away into darkness and disorder.

86 : 6. In all thy prayers let thy heart be without the words, rather than thy words without the heart.

89 : "Mercy of the Lord."
    "I will sing of the mercies of the Lord forever." V. 1.
    "Mercy shall be built up forever." V. 2.
    "Mercy shall go before Thy face." V. 14.
    "My mercy shall be with him." V. 24.
    "My mercy will I keep for him forevermore." V. 28.

90 : 12. "So teach us to number our days that we may apply our hearts unto wisdom." St. Augustine says we will never do that unless we number every day as our last day.

The last day is hidden that every day may be heeded.

"I expect to pass through this world but once. If, therefore, there be any kindness I can show, any good I can do, any help I can give, let me do it now : let me not defer it or neglect it, for I will not pass this way again."

91 : The believer's security. Vs. 1–12.
His victory. V. 13.
His exaltation. Vs. 14, 15.
His eternal satisfaction. V. 16.
Saints are safe— "Surely He shall deliver thee from the snare . . . and from the noisome pestilence." V. 3.
The evil is limited — "Only with thine eyes shalt thou . . . see the reward of the wicked." V. 8.
The Lord has reasons for preserving his own — "Because thou hast made the Lord, my refuge, the Most High, thy habitation." V. 9.

4. The feathers of God's wings are his tender mercies. See Psalm 145 : 9.

91 : 11, 12. Satan's version— Presumptuousness.
Christ's version — Trustfulness.

14–16. Seven things God will do for the believer : —
"I will deliver him." Vs. 14, 15.
"I will set him on high." V. 14.
"I will answer his call." V. 15.
"I will be with him in trouble." V. 15.
"I will honor him." V. 15.

"I will satisfy him." V. 16.
"I will show him my salvation." V. 16.

92 : 7. The wicked flourish to become fuel.

14. The righteous flourish for fruit.

94 : 13. Grace withereth without adversity. The devil is but God's master-fencer, to teach us to handle our weapons.

96 : 6. Some people say there is no need of beauty in God's sanctuary; you should use the money for the heathen — meaning themselves.

97 : 2. God's government is often mysterious, yet always righteous.

101 : Years ago a prince of Saxe-Gotha, whenever he thought that one of his ministers or judges was not what he ought to be, used always to send him Ps. 101 to read.

103 : The mercy of God.
Its quality — "tender." V. 4.
Its measure — "plenteous." V. 8.
Its extent — as high as heaven. V. 11.
Its duration — "from everlasting to everlasting." V. 17.

13. Fatherly pity — filial fear.

105 : 37. "He brought them forth with silver and gold: and there was not one feeble person among their tribes." Wealthy and healthy.

106 : They believed and sang. V. 12.
They believed not and murmured. Vs. 24, 25.

106 : 15. Fat in body — lean in soul. See Psalm 78 : 31.

107 : Note the contrasts : —

    No city to dwell in. V. 4. — A city of habitation. V. 7.

    Hungry, thirsty, faint. V. 5. — Satisfied and filled. V. 9.

    Caused to wander. V. 7. — Led forth. V. 40

    Sit in darkness. V. 10. — Brought out of darkness. V. 14.

    Bound in affliction and iron V. 10. — He brake their bands in sunder. V. 14.

    Draw near to death. V. 18. — He saveth out of distresses. V. 19.

    Go down to the sea. V. 23. — Bringeth to the desired haven. V. 30.

    Commandeth and raiseth stormy wind. V. 25. — Maketh the storm a calm. V. 29.

  19. Free grace is a harbor into which few ships run, except through stress of weather. Till the end of the creature is reached, men will not seek the Creator.

116 : A Christian's experience : —

    Conviction — "I found trouble and sorrow." V. 3.

    Prayer — "O Lord, I beseech thee, deliver my soul." V. 4.

    Gratitude — "What shall I render unto the Lord for all his benefits?" V. 12.

    Assurance — "O Lord I am thy servant." V. 16.

116 : 16. Freedom under Christ — "Thou hast loosed my bonds."

117 : 2. "The truth of the Lord endureth forever." "I am the truth."

119 : 18. Disciple's *prayer.* " Hide not thy commandments from me."

Promise. "I will instruct thee and teach thee." Ps. 32 : 8.

Fulfilment. "Then opened he their understanding, that they might understand the Scriptures." Luke 24 : 45.

31. "I have *stuck* unto thy testimonies." The best law for Bible study is perseverance, sticking-to.

59, 60. The prodigal son's epitaph.
Thinking for himself.
Thinking about himself.
Practical and prompt.

71. It is a good wave that washes the mariner on to the rock.

94. Profession — "I am thine ; "
Prayer — "save me , "
Plea — "for I have sought thy precepts."
" Thine," — by purchase, surrender.
" Save me " — from sin, error, enemies, carelessness, temptation, self.

105. "Thy word is a lamp unto my feet" — to walk by ; not to our tongues to talk about.

114. "Thou art my hiding-place." Hidden *in* Him, never *from* Him.

136. Bendetti, a Franciscan monk, author of "Stabat Mater," one day was found weeping, and when asked the reason of his tears, replied, "I weep because Love goes about unloved."

166. Trust and obedience. "Lord, I have hoped for thy salvation, and done thy commandments."

121 : 4. Let not any think that the devil is now dead — no , nor yet asleep. As "He that keepeth Israel," so he that hateth Israel, "neither slumbereth nor sleepeth."

A poor woman in the East was robbed in the night. The sultan asked, "Why did you sleep?" "Because I thought you never slept."

Alexander the Great told his soldiers, "I wake that you may sleep."

5. The Lord is thy keeper — day and night, in and out, forever.

122 : 6 Wherever thou canst send a thought, God can command a blessing.

125 : 1, 2. As the Lord encircles his people like a mountain-rampart, he must be removed before they can be removed. Hence, "Stand fast in the Lord." Phil. 4 : 1.

131 : 1. Present.
   2. Past.
   3. Future.

138 : 6. Pride never prepares a man for Paradise, but for perdition.

140 : 5. The net is "*by* the wayside;" there is no danger *in* the way.

141 : 7, 8. "Our bones are scattered at the grave's mouth, as when one cutteth and cleaveth wood upon the earth. But mine eyes are unto Thee, O God the Lord: in Thee is my trust; leave not my soul destitute."

These texts are inscribed on the cross which marks the site of the well into which the dead bodies were dropped every night during the siege of Cawnpore, 1857 — (preceding the massacre of Cawnpore, in which about one thousand Europeans were murdered).

143 : Full of prayers — "Hear!" "give ear!" "answer!" etc.

5. Remembrance — meditation — musing upon. The works of God's hands cause eager desire and thirst.

145 : 14. Lifting up.

15. Looking up.

17. What the Lord is — "righteous in all his ways, and holy in all his works."

18. Where the Lord is — "nigh unto all them that call upon him, to all that call upon him in truth."

19. What the Lord will do — "He will fulfil the desire of them that fear him: he also will hear their cry, and will save them."

150: The most complete directory of praise: —
    V. 1. Whom shall we praise? Where?
    V. 2. Why?
    V. 3–5. Wherewith? (Whatever is most helpful.)
    V. 6. Who shall praise?

PROVERBS.

When a young man said to Carlyle that there was nothing in the Book of Proverbs, he replied: "Make a few proverbs and you will think differently of the book."

He that would be wise, let him read Proverbs. He that would be holy, let him read Psalms.

1:22. Simple ones — scorners — fools.
    V. 25. They "would none of my reproof."
    V. 30. "They would none of my counsel."
    "Israel would none of me." Ps. 81:11.

32. Bacon said, "Prosperity doth best discover vice, but adversity doth best discover virtue."

4:18. I am walking toward a great light, and the nearer I get, the brighter it is.

The last words from Longfellow's pen : —

> "Out of the shadows of night,
> The world rolls into light :
>   It is *day-break everywhere.*"

When St. Cuthbert was overtaken in a terrible storm, his companions said to him, "The sea is before us, and the path behind us is blocked with snow. What shall we do?" He replied, "Thank God, the road to heaven is not obstructed"

6 : 22. Shall lead — shall keep — shall talk.

7 : 18–20. Like a faithless wife, the world takes advantage of the Lord's absence to seek guilty pleasure; but this can only last till his return. On the other hand, the Lord's return ends his people's sorrows and brings them holy and everlasting joy.

8 : 34. Willing, watching, waiting.

10 : 7. "The memory of the just is blessed."

"Only the actions of the just
Smell sweet and blossom in their dust."

22. The blessings we enjoy are not the fruit of our own merit, but the fruit of God's mercy.

13 : 15. "The way of transgressors is *hard*," because,—
(1.) Sin begets sin;
(2.) it makes a guilty conscience;
(3.) it always turns out hideous;
(4.) it brings future punishment.

24. Better the child cry than the father sigh.

14 : 12. The cream of earth's pleasures floats on the top. He that thinks by a deeper draught to find yet more, fares worse.

15 : 16. Some things come to the poor that can't get into the doors of the rich, whose money blocks the way: peace, contentment, etc.

16 : 18. Be humble or you'll stumble.

17 : 17. A true friend is like ivy — the greater the ruin, the closer he clings.

18 : 24. We have not to hold on to Christ; he *sticks* to us.

22 : 6. Happy are they who learn their first lessons in their mother's arms!

Children old enough to sin are old enough to repent.

Satan does not wait till the children grow up;— why should you?

28 : 1. If Christians should shrink back at every contrary wind that blows, they would never make their voyage to heaven.

ECCLESIASTES.

9 : 10. Better say, "This one thing I do," than to say, "These fifty things I dabble in."

12 : 1. God prizes a Christian in the bud, and delights in the blossoms of youth more than in the sheddings of old age.

Usually where the devil pleads antiquity, he retains possession.

As there are none so old that they need despair of mercy, so there are none so young that they should presume on mercy.

Youthful sins lay a foundation for aged sorrows.

12 : 6. Pierson makes this verse set forth four ways of death: —

    a. Silver cord loosed — spinal cord loosed — paralysis.
    b. Golden bowl broken — the skull and brain.
    c. Pitcher broken — lungs — asphyxia.
    d. Wheel at cistern broken — heart — syncope.

SONG OF SOLOMON.

2 : 10. The experience of the believer who has found an all-sufficiency in Christ.

   15. Little foxes that spoil the vines : —
      Selfishness spoils love.
      Discontent spoils joy.
      Anxious thought spoils peace.
      Impatience spoils longsuffering.
      Bitter words spoil gentleness.
      Indolence spoils goodness.
      Doubt spoils faith.
      Pride spoils meekness.
      Love of pleasure spoils temperance.

8 : 5. Leaning, not leading.

ISAIAH.

1 : 2–4. A tenfold accusation: —
    1. Children have rebelled against God. V. 2.
    2. Israel doth not know. V. 3.
    3. My people doth not consider. V. 3.
    4. A sinful nation. V. 4.
    5. A people laden with iniquity. V. 4.
    6. A seed of evil-doers. V. 4.
    7. Children that are corrupters. V. 4.

ISAIAH.

   8. They have forsaken the Lord. V. 4.
   9. They have provoked the Holy One of Israel to anger. V. 4.
   10. They are gone away backward. V. 4.

6. "From the sole of the foot even unto the head there is no soundness." Most people would do like the African princess who broke the looking-glass because she was so ugly.

Civilization is a poor varnish. You have only to scratch it to turn up the same old egotism that has prevailed six thousand years.

16, 17. An eight-fold instruction: —
   1. Wash you, make you clean. V. 16.
   2. Put away the evil of your doings. V. 16.
   3. Cease to do evil. V. 16.
   4. Lean to do well. V. 17.
   5. Seek judgment. V. 17.
   6. Relieve the oppressed. V. 17.
   7. Judge the fatherless. V. 17.
   8. Plead for the widow. V. 17.

18. No matter how fast the color is, the blood of Jesus Christ can wash it out.

6 : 1. Uzziah's reign was a kind of Victorian era in Jewish history. It was when this passed away into shame and disgrace that Isaiah saw the Eternal King on his throne.

22 : 22. The Spanish Jews have a silver key of David, bearing the inscription, "God shall open, the King shall enter."

26 : 3. P. P. Bliss used to say, "I love this verse more than any other verse in the Bible, 'Thou wilt keep him in perfect peace whose mind is stayed on Thee: because he trusteth in Thee.'"

The tree of peace strikes its roots into the crevices of the Rock of Ages.

33 : This chapter is true literally of Sennacherib's invasion.

21. Jerusalem lacked a river, and nearly all large cities are built on seas or rivers. The Lord promised to be a river without the drawback that enemies' vessels could come up against the city. So there is no drawback, no temptation in any blessing the Lord gives.

40 : Nine aspects of man's insufficiency : —
   V. 6. Grass, flower of field.
   V. 15. Drop, small dust, a very little thing.
   V. 17. Nothing, less than nothing, vanity.
   V. 22. Grasshoppers.

6–8. The frailty of human life. Ps. 103 : 15, 16 ; Matt. 6 : 30 ; Luke 12 : 28 ; 1 Peter 1 : 24.
   In its short life. Ps. 90 : 6 ; James 1 : 11.
   In its full-blown glory. V. 6.
   In its sure decay. V. 7 ; 1 Peter 1 : 24.
The permanence of God's Word. Mark 13 : 31 ; 1 Peter 1 : 25 ; Ps 119 : 89.
   Proclaimed among men. Col. 1 : 23.
   Centered in the gospel. 1 Peter 1 : 25.

31. I never could understand the order — mount up, run, walk, — until I saw a man riding a bicycle.

It is easy to mount, but to walk or go slowly takes a clever rider. So with a convert.

41 : 10. Fear and despair are high points of atheism.

42 : 6. Called — held — kept — used.

One day Miss F. R. Havergal asked her attendant to read this verse : "I the Lord have called thee in righteousness, and will hold thine hand, and will keep thee." "Well," she said, "I will just go home on that"—and she died that day.

43 : 2. "Where is Jesus of Nazareth, my old and faithful friend?" asked Jonathan Edwards, dying, "I know He will be with me." And he died triumphant.

45 : 7. "I create evil"—not sin, but the punishment thereof.

53 : Notice the paradoxes : —

Despised, yet accepted and adored.

Poor, yet rich.

To die, yet to live.

The Rabbis said there must be a double Messiah to fulfil this chapter.

2. In the sight of God, a tender plant; in the sight of man, a root out of a dry ground.

55 : 7. God is angry with the wicked. Isa. 63 : 9, 10; Eze. 22 : 21, 22.

God is unwilling to punish. 2 Peter 3 : 9; Eze. 33 : 11 ; Jonah 4 : 11.

God is glad to forgive. Isa. 1 : 18 ; 1 John 2 : 1. 2.

God rejoices over the forgiven. Luke 15 : 6, 7, 22, 24 ; Isa. 62 : 3, 5.

59 : 1. If our water-supply runs short, I do not conclude that the river or lake has run dry, but that our pipes are out of order.

62 : 2. "By a new name":—
Saints, because of their holiness.
Believers, because of their faith.
Brethren, because of their love.
Disciples, because of their knowledge.
Christians, because of their head.

65 : 24. "And it shall come to pass that before they call, I will answer." God sometimes answers before we ask!

JEREMIAH.

1 : 11. The almond blossoms before any other tree. Hence —speed, haste. V. 12.

8 : 7. The Persians formed their almanacs by the movements of the storks.
    a. Birds mingle music with work.
    b. They fly high when migrating.
    c. They know when to start.
    d. All the family goes together.

16 : 2. Jeremiah was the only man in the Bible who was told not to marry.

17 : 8. Strong faith can live in any climate.

18 : The story of the potter and his clay.

Three men in the Bible whom God made up again : —
- Jacob, after Bethel, fell into double dealing, but God met him again at the fords of Jabbok. So business men restored.
- Simon Peter denied Christ, but Christ said to him, "Feed my sheep." So ministers restored.
- Mark started with Paul and Barnabas, but went back; yet God made him up again into the friend of Peter (1 Peter 5 : 13). So can backsliders be restored.

Man differs from clay; he can resist his Maker. See Isa. 45 : 9.

LAMENTATIONS.

3 : 27. It is hard to cast off the devil's yoke when we have worn it long upon our necks.

EZEKIEL.

5 : 5. The Rabbis said that Jerusalem was the actual center of the earth, and in the church of the Holy Sepulcher is a large stone that marks the exact center.

11 : 16. Israel, though dispersed, would find God even among the heathen.

17 : 54. Some Christians are a "comfort" to the worldly.

33 : 3. Four trumpet calls : —
Beware. Eze. 33 : 3; Num. 10 : 5.

Be glad. Num. 10 : 10.
Be useful. Rev. 8 : 6.
Be ready. Eze. 7 : 14 ; 1 Cor. 15 : 52.

34 : 10–29. Notice the "I will's" of the Lord God on behalf of his sheep.

The Shepherd and the sheep : —
V. 11. I will search them and seek them out.
V. 12. I will deliver them.
V. 13. I will bring them out.
V. 13. I will gather them together.
V. 13. I will bring them in.
V. 14. I will feed them.
V. 15. I will cause them to lie down.
V. 16. I will bind up the broken.
V. 16. I will strengthen the sick.

14. There are a good many lean sheep in God's fold, but none in his pasture.

37 : 2. Many a preacher fails because he does not visit his people and find out their actual condition.
Survey the ground where sin and death reign.

4. Preaching to dry bones!
9. Preaching to the wind!

DANIEL.

Nothing derogatory is recorded of Samuel, Jonathan, or Daniel, yet they were not sinless, but confessed their sins.

1 : 8. Boy heroes. By reason of their purpose God gave them —

  a. Favor and tender love with the prince.
  b. Health and comeliness of features.
  c. Knowledge and skill in learning and wisdom.
  d. Pre-eminence.
 Don't eat the king's fare; don't go with the tide if it is wrong.

12. Don't be afraid to test your theories.

15. Purity pays. He who abstains from drinking, smoking, etc., always has the more comely features.

5 : 27. Weighed and found wanting : —
  a. The moralist — morality, integrity, uprightness.
  b. The formalist — ritual, outward prosperity.
  c. The worldling — riches, business, pleasure.

9 : 5–15. Notice the different ways of expressing sin : —
 We have sinned. Vs. 5, 8, 11, 15.
  " " committed iniquity. V. 5.
  " " done wickedly. V. 5.
  " " rebelled (by departing from precepts and judgments). Vs. 5, 9.
 We have not hearkened unto thy servants the prophets. V. 6.
 We have trespassed. V. 7.
  " " been disobedient. V. 10, 11.
  " " transgressed. V. 11.
  " " neglected to pray. V. 13.

HOSEA

9 : 10. Under the old covenant God set his laws before his people; under the new, he promised to put them into our hearts. See Heb. 10 : 16.

7 : 13–15. God's seven-fold charge against Ephraim.
    Fled from God. V. 13.
    Transgressed against God. V. 13.
    Spoken lies against God. V. 13.
    Not cried to God with the heart. V. 14.
    Assembled for corn and wine. V. 14.
    Rebel against God. V. 14.
    Imagined mischief against God. V. 15.

11 : 3. Guidance step by step.

AMOS.

4 : 12. "Prepare to meet thy God." Four things in this text:—
    a. There is one God.
    b. We are accountable to him.
    c. We must meet him.
    d. We need preparation to meet him.

JONAH.

1 : 3. It is impossible to flee from God's presence. Ps. 139 : 7. Give up the vain attempt to-day. Jonah "paid his fare" and never got it refunded. Sin is an expensive business. He took the wrong boat — the wrong track.

1 : 4. Disobedience always leads us into troubled waters.

5. The want of pardon is the only spring of a servile man's duty. He plies his prayers as sailors do the pumps — only in a storm, or when fearful of sinking.

11. Sin in the soul is like Jonah in the ship. It turns the smoothest water into a tempestuous sea.

13, 14. The unavailing efforts of the Mediterranean oarsman have their counterpart, —
    a. In our efforts to convert others.
    b. " "   "   "   " our families.
    c. " "   "   "   " ourselves.
The cure is — Cry to God.

3 : 2. After all the delay and discipline, Jonah had to go back to his first starting-place.

4 : 7. Unbelief in the heart is like the worm in Jonah's gourd — an unseen adversary.

MICAH.

The Rod in Micah : —
    5 : 1. Upon the Saviour ; cf. Lam. 3 : 1.
    6 : 9. Upon the sinner ; cf. Ps. 2 : 9.
    7 : 14. Upon the saint ; cf. Ps. 23 : 4.

6 : 8. A trinity of precepts : —
    Do justly.
    Love mercy.
    Walk humbly with thy God.

NAHUM.

1: 2. Of the thirty Roman Emperors and Governors who persecuted Christians, not one came to a peaceful end.

HABAKKUK.

2 : Five woes against five common sins: —
Unsatiableness. V. 5.
Covetousness. V. 9.
Cruelty. V. 12.
Drunkenness. V. 15.
Idolatry. V. 18.

ZEPHANIAH.

3 : 9. There are only two newspapers published in Palestine to-day (1894), and both of them are in Hebrew.

ZECHARIAH.

Christ — The Branch. Chapter 3 : 8.
Priest and King. " 6 : 13.
Just and Lowly. " 9 : 9.
A Fountain. " 13 : 1.
The Shepherd. " 13 : 7.

3 : V. 4. Cleansed.
Clothed.
V. 5. Crowned.

MALACHI.

2 : 5–7. The characteristics of a true minister : —
  a. Fearing God — his state of mind.

  b. Proclaiming the truth — his message.
  c. Avoiding iniquity — his purpose.
  d. Walking with God — his habit.
  e. Turning men to God — his work.
  f. Teaching the law of God — his duty.
  g. Acting as God's messenger — his commission.

3 : 3. The refiner sits watching until his own image is reflected in the metal. Job. 23 : 10.

> "But that thy fires may surely burn
> All sordid, sensual dross away,
> Lord at the furnace watch and yearn
> Till from the silver's heart return
> Thine image pure as day.

> "O teach us lowly to remain
> Without one murmur at thy feet,
> Nor at the heaviest cross complain,
> Till thou each docile spirit train
> Into thy will complete."

 8. Men try to rob God of their time by desecrating the Sabbath by toiling; but they die off younger.

 17. White clouds are drawn up by the sun from swamps and stagnant pools.

 The church is "the pearl" (Matt. 13 : 45), and individuals are "jewels."

4 : 2. How many men and women who were doomed to a life of poverty, monotony, and toil which almost amounts to slavery, have been translated by experience of the love of Christ out of darkness into wondrous light. The grave has been transformed into the gate of glory. How many men

and women, themselves apparently lost and dragging others to ruin, have been arrested and converted and transfigured so as to become like the wings of a dove covered with silver, and her feathers with yellow gold.

NEW TESTAMENT.

MATTHEW.

"Kingdom of heaven"—used thirty-two times in Matthew.

Sixty-five quotations from the Old Testament.

In the first two chapters the evangelist sees the fulfilment of five prophecies.

Two genealogies of our Lord:—
> Matthew, the first: a king must have a genealogy.
> Mark, none: all a servant needs is character.
> Luke, the second: a perfect man must have one.
> John, none: God needs none.

1:23. "They shall call his name Emmanuel . . . God with us." This gospel closes with the promise—"Lo, I am with you alway!"—Emmanuel.

2: 1. "Bethlehem" means "house of bread." Out of Bethlehem came the "Bread of Life."

2. God caught the magi with a star, the fishermen with a fish.

Wise men—philosophers—were the *first* who came to worship Christ.

13. Obedience requires sometimes activity—"flee;" sometimes patient waiting—"be thou there."

2 : 14. Even in his infancy Christ suffered for us.
God sent one man into the world without sin, but none without sorrow.

3 : 2. We do n't believe in a dry-eyed faith; repentance is the tear in the eye of faith.

5. Sensational preaching.

11, 12. Those baptized with fire escape burning by fire.

16. The first time the Spirit rested upon man!
A dove the emblem of peace.   Gen. 8: 11.
Of harmlessness.   Matt. 10: 16.
Of purity.   Song of Solomon 6: 9.
Of beauty.   Ps. 68: 13.

4 : 5. The devil sets most of us on a pinnacle of self-confidence so that we fall.

7. "It is written *again*." Do not blot out one passage of Scripture, but set another alongside of it. The Bible is self interpreting. John 19 : 37.
God must be trusted, not tempted.

11. The first Adam was tempted in a garden, and fell: The second Adam in a wilderness, and he came off victorious.

19. If you would be fishers of men, you must leave your old nets.

5 : The Law was given on a mountain to a man of God. The Law was expounded on a mountain by the Son of God.

5 : 5. A missionary in Jamaica asked a little black boy, "Who are the meek?" He answered, "Those who give soft answers to rough questions."

8. You must pass through the narrow gate of purity before you can see the King.

11. Who would shake those trees upon which there is no fruit?

13, 14. Salt to preserve, and light to guide. Both silent in action but great in effect.

14. Poor world! What a faint light it receives from most Christians!

The lighthouse, if its light is not burning, is a peril instead of a safeguard.

Men do not stumble when the lamp shines brightly.

16. It is not you that is to shine, but your light. The moon shines by reflected light. A diamond is dull in the dark.

The brighter the light, the less people remark about the lamp.

The light abides pure, though the air be corrupted in which it shines.

20. Soul-justifying Saviour.
Self-justifying scribes.

28. There may be guests in the house, although they look not out of the windows. So there may be lust in the heart of a man when his outward life seems pure

5 : 38. To rise above simple justice is a great question, not of education, but of sanctification.

44. To do evil for good is human corruption.
To do good for good is civil retribution.
To do good for evil is Christian perfection.

Plutarch said, "A man should not allow himself to hate even his enemies, because if you indulge this passion on some occasions, it will rise of itself on others. If you hate your enemies, you will contract such a vicious habit of mind, as by degrees will break out upon those who are your friends, or those who are indifferent to you."

Never contract a friendship with a man that is not better than thyself — this was Confucius's advice regarding friendship.

46. As an echo returns the voice it receives, so many will return a kindness when kindness is shown.

48. We have got a good many Christians who are good in spots, but mighty poor in other spots.

The serene beauty of a holy life is the most powerful influence in the world, next to the might of God.

6 : 1. "Take heed that ye do not your alms before men, to be seen of them : otherwise ye have no reward of your Father which is in heaven."

He who desires honor is not worthy of honor.

The harp sounds sweetly, yet it hears not its own melody.

Good ends do not make bad actions lawful, yet bad ends make good actions sinful.

If some bestow a little money on the repairs of a church, it must be recorded in glazed windows.

Where self is the end of our actions, Satan (not God) is the rewarder of them.

He that traffics in God's service in order to procure men's praises, suffers shipwreck in the haven and loses his wages.

6 : 2. *Hypocrisy.*

The gospel professed may lift a man to heaven: but only the gospel possessed will bring him into heaven.

We need not sound a trumpet for anything we bestow: for when the last trumpet shall sound, every work will be revealed.

Saints should be like spire-steeples, smallest where they are highest.

Religion is the best armor a man can have, but the worst cloak.

Hypocrites are like looking-glasses which present the faces that are not in them.

The hypocrite would not put on the appearance of virtue and religion if it was not the most proper means to gain love.

14. Christ said, "Forgive to be forgiven."

Paul said, "Forgive because forgiven." Eph. 4 : 32.

16. It is both meat and drink to a formalist to fast if others do but see him. Some professors are like hens that no sooner drop their eggs than they begin to chatter.

6:26. Object lessons: fowls, lilies, grass, foxes, raven, etc.

The river of God's truth flows down before us pure and clear as crystal, but we take our theological stick and stir it up, until you cannot see the bottom Oh, for the simplicity of Christ in all our instructions — the simplicity He practised when standing among the people, He took a lily, and said, "There is a lesson of the manner I will clothe you;" and, pointing to a raven, said, "There is a lesson of the way I will feed you; consider the lilies — behold the fowls of the air."

Providence — that does the housework of the universe; busy, kindly, thoughtful, the hospitable word, that makes things ready for us, cares for all our life, busies itself about us, and that says to us, "The very hairs of your head are all numbered!"

7: In this chapter we have: —
Two gates — strait, and wide;
Two ways — broad, and narrow;
Two classes — many, and few;
Two destinations — life, and destruction
Two trees — good, and corrupt;
Two fruits — good, and evil;
Two things done to trees — hewn down, and cast out;
Two houses;
Two foundations — rock, and sand;
Two builders — wise, and foolish;

MATTHEW.

Two storms;
Two results — the one house stood, the other fell.

7 : 2. He that blows into a heap of dust is in danger of putting out his own eyes.

7. Many pray like boys who knock at doors and then run away.

13. If a man goes into the evil way, the great enemy of souls goes after him and blots out his footprints.

16. "Shake the tree," said Luther, "and you will see if there is any fruit"
When the wheels of a clock move within, the hands on the dial move without.

19. If ye be not fruit-bearing plants, ye will become burning brands.

24. Build on the Rock, and fear no shock.
"Upon a rock." R. V. : "upon *the* rock." A bed of limestone underlies all Palestine, and Christ speaks of the man who digged down to it.

8 :   Four typical miracles : —
Leprosy, typifying guilt.
Palsy, " impotence.
Fever, " passion.
Demoniacy, " slavery of sin.

10. Christ marveled at unbelief. Mark 6 : 6.
How is it ye have no faith ?   " 4 : 40.
Oh, thou of little faith.   Matt. 14 : 31.

Great is thy faith. Matt. 15 : 28.
So great faith. " 8 : 10.

8 : 17. The key to Christ's atoning death : "Himself took our infirmities and bare our sicknesses."

24. "He was asleep" — Christ's humanity.

26. "He rebuked the winds" — His divinity.

25. Lord — We. }
Save — Perish. }
When a man really wants the Saviour, he does not need any one to teach him how to pray.

9 : 9. It was a great victory to win a promising business man.

36. What are the "multitudes" that Jesus sees to-day, from his throne in glory? Eight hundred millions heathen, two hundred millions Mohammedans, etc.

10 : 8. The motive — free grace. }
The measure — free giving. }
The Christian's commission — "Raise the dead."
How? "Go, preach." V. 7.
Who are the dead? All. 1 Cor. 15 : 22.
Why are they "dead"? Because they are "alienated from God." Eph. 4 : 18.
To what to be raised? To "sit together in heavenly places in Christ Jesus." Eph. 2 : 6.

9. Faith is better than funds for the life that now is, and for the life that is to come.

38. A saint is often under a cross; never under a curse.

11 : 29. The eastern yoke is made for two necks. If Christ is with us, we are blessed. There is no room for a third neck. 2 Cor. 6 : 14.

The only description of Christ's heart —"lowly."

The burden of law remains eternally the same, but the inspiration of grace enables men to bear it.

    Something to do — "Come unto me."
    Something to take — His yoke.
    Something to leave — Your burden.
    Something to find — Rest.

"Learn of me." If the life of Christ be not your pattern, the death of Christ will never be your pardon. What He was by nature, we should be by grace.

30. He that deems the yoke of Christ heavy, will not find his crown easy.

When Christ takes the burden of guilt off a sinner's shoulders, He places the yoke of obedience upon his neck.

12 : 31. Those who think they have committed the unpardonable sin seldom worry themselves about other sins.

45. If godly sorrow takes possession of the house, it will quickly shut sin out.

13 : 23. Understanding the Word with the heart (v. 15) is the result of the Spirit's dealing, and indicates regeneration. 1 Cor. 2 : 10, 16.

45. The "pearl of great price" is the church. Jesus Christ is the merchantman and gave all to purchase the pearl. Could not pay a higher price. Not "pearls," but the "pearl." Brought from great depths, into changed surroundings, at risk of diver's life; noted for purity; no need of polishing; perfect when found.

The church is the pearl. Believers are "jewels."

14 : 4. John the Baptist was an uncompromising preacher.

9. The head of John the Baptist was a high price for a few moments' entertainment.

31. "O thou of little faith, wherefore didst thou doubt?" Peter had enough faith to keep him from drowning, but not from doubting.

15 :   The woman's faith overcame His —
Silence. V. 23.
Sovereignty. V. 24.
Severity. V. 26.

25. Christ heard the woman when she dropped the title, "Son of David" (v. 22). She was a Gentile.

A prayer of three links, connecting earth with heaven: "Lord — Help — Me."

27. Don't be satisfied with crumbs. Go for the whole loaf.

16 : 13–17. The answers of opinion and of revelation. Why did Jesus come into the world? 1 John 3 : 5, 8; John 1 : 29; 1 Tim. 1 : 15; Luke 19 : 10, etc.

13. It makes a great difference to men what they think of Jesus.

16 : 15. It makes less difference to a man what others think of Jesus than what he thinks.

16. A great confession. }
22. A great collapse.

22, 23. The devil hates to consider the death of Jesus, knowing that it is so important.

26. The devil gained the whole world and lost his soul. Who would change places with him?

Pleasure, Profit, and Preferment are the wicked man's trinity: and his carnal self is these in unity.

17 : 2. The law was given with thunderings, lightnings, and darkness. Christ was manifested in glory and peace.

5. "This is my beloved Son, in whom I am well pleased; hear ye him." God here quotes three Old Testament texts:—

a. This is my beloved Son. Ps. 2:7.
b. In whom I am well pleased. Isa. 42:1.
c. Hear ye him. Deut. 18:15.

This was the last time God spoke to men.

He who refuses to hear the voice of Jesus Christ shall never see his face.

18 : 3. "As little children." Not foolish, not playful; but gentle, obedient, truthful, pure, trusting.

5. The pastor who leads the lambs will be able to lead the sheep. Every time you lay your hand on a child's head, you lay it on his mother's heart.

18 : 7. He that sins is weak; but he that leads others into sin is devilish.

19 : 21. "If thou wilt be perfect, go and sell that thou hast, and give to the poor, and thou shalt have treasure in heaven: and come and follow me."
It was the force of these words that moved Francis of Assisi to give up the world and become the power he was in the Church.

22. Wealth is no harm: but the inability to give it up is deadly.

23. Christian men often become rich, but rich men seldom become Christians.

28. Now the world judges the godly. Hereafter the godly shall judge the world.

20 : 27. A humble saint looks most like a citizen of heaven.

21 : 37. Men would never have known that they would put God to death, unless Christ had been born.

23 : 27. Whitewashed, not washed white in the blood.
Some very good-looking people are deformed on the inside.

24 : 2. John does not mention the destruction of Jerusalem, as he wrote after it had taken place.

18. In the ruins of Pompeii there was found the petrified body of a woman in the act of snatching her jewels.

22. "The elect" are the "whosoever will's": the "non-elect" are the "whosoever wont's."

24 : 42. The Lord's exhortations to holiness are never based on the fear of death, but on the hope of his return, and its unexpectedness.

We know the duty ("watch"), but not the day.

47. The promotion God gives is not like earthly promotion, wherein the eminence of one excludes that of another — but rather like the diffusion of love in which the more each has, the more there is for all.

49. Unkindness to the Lord's people, and fellowship with the ungodly, are two great marks of hypocrites.

25 : 15. Many thousands of watchsprings can be made out of a pound of iron. See that you improve faithfully the talent God has given you.

21. Not "well done good and *successful*" servant, but "*faithful*" servant.

God has three kinds of servants in the world — (1) slaves, who serve him from a principle of fear; (2) hirelings, who serve him for the sake of wages; (3) sons, who serve him under the influence of love.

34. The Church was chosen before the foundation of the world. Eph. 1:4; Titus 1:2. The Jews (here) "from the foundation of the world."

35. Many love at their tongue's end; but the godly love at their fingers' end.

26 : 20. The Lord's Supper is a memorial of a departed Friend, a prophecy of a returning Friend, and a parable of a present Friend.

26 : 56. Christ's circle gradually narrowed down. First, the multitudes left him; then, many so-called disciples, lastly, the twelve.

27 : Christ's innocence attested by:—
Judas. V. 4.
Pilate's wife. V. 19.
Pilate. V. 24.
Herod. Luke 23 : 15.
Thief. Luke 23 : 41.
Centurion. Luke 23 : 47.

33. On Golgotha there were skulls of all sizes.

35. The soldiers took from Jesus his garments, but He laid aside the robe of flesh of his own will.

36. Twelve views of the cross. Luke 23 : 48.
The soldiers saw in Christ a criminal, with cruelty.
The women saw in Christ a benefactor, with sorrow.
His mother saw in Christ a son, with anguish.
The disciples saw in Christ blighted hopes, with perplexity.
The first thief saw in Christ a malefactor, with hardness.
The second thief saw in Christ a King, with penitence.
The centurion saw in Christ divinity, with conviction.
The priests saw in Christ an impostor, with mockery.

Angels saw in Christ love, with wonder.
Devils saw in Christ the seed of woman, with dismay.
Jehovah saw in Christ obedience, with affection.
The passers-by saw in Christ nothing, with indifference.

The cross cannot be explained. To nail our poor theories on that tree but shows how our love has cooled and stiffened and expired.

57. None of the Gospels forget to mention Joseph of Arimathæa.

63. Christ's enemies remembered what his disciples forgot: "We remember that that deceiver said, while he was yet alive, After three days, I will rise again."

28 : 19, 20. "Go ye . . . I am with you." In other words, "Come with me to this work."

God only had one Son, and he sent him on a foreign mission.

MARK.

Christ, the servant, goes about his work at once.

1 : 22. There is an awful possibility of being "astonished," without being convinced, persuaded, saved.

23. A devil in a synagogue!

30. The French for mother-in-law is "belle-mère"— beautiful mother.

Suffering everywhere:—

   In the synagogue. V. 23.
   In the home. V. 30.
   In the city. V. 32.
  But Christ is there too.

2: 1. If Christ is in the house, your neighbors will soon know it.

3. Four men thought it worth while to bring one man to Christ.

4. They thought it more important to get to Christ than to have an orderly meeting.

5. Christ saw not their "perseverance" or "ingenuity," but their "faith."
 Christ's coming —
  Awakens hope, effort.
  Brings pardon, power.
  Calls forth praise.

6. A new religion provoked opposition. Formality versus Will of God.

8. To know the hearts of men was, with the Jews, a test of the true Messiah's claims. See Isa. 11 : 3.

9. The true character of a miracle : the outward manifestation of the power of God, in order that we may believe in the power of God in things that are invisible.

11. "Thy sins be forgiven thee. . . . Arise and walk." A separate miracle,— being healed. So to-day, a drunkard may be forgiven, but he does not at

once recover his steady hands, etc. The spiritual miracle must come *first*. Matt. 6 : 33.

17. Christ, the Great Physician.
How do we know when people are sick in mind? in body? in soul?
What is the medicine? Prisons, hospitals, etc.
Who are sick in soul? Isa. 1 : 6 ; 1 John 1 : 7.

23–28. Withered hearts.
3 : 1– 5. Withered hand.

3. "Stand forth"— as a confession of need.
5. "Stretch forth"— as a confession of faith.

4. These are indeed obstinate in their infidelity who, when they can say nothing against a truth, will say nothing for it; and when they cannot resist, yet will not yield.

5. Every conversion is a miracle. The sinner can no more "believe" than this man could raise his withered hand, without power being given from on high.

6. Christ's enemies.
7–12. Christ's friends.
13–19. Christ's messengers.

13. Chosen,
Bought,
Planted,
 that they should bear fruit.

3 : 28–30. The unpardonable sin: A union of light in the head and hatred in the heart. Not a sin of ignorance or presumption, but of defiance.

4 : 26. The seed passed through seven stages: (1) cast into the ground; (2) springing up; (3) growing; (4) blade; (5) ear; (6) full corn in the ear; (7) harvest.

28. Blade of thought.
Green ear of conviction.
Full ear of faith.
Christ overcomes the storm, chap. 4 : 39;
> the devil, 5 : 13;
> disease, 5 : 29;
> death, 5 : 42.

5 : Devils prayed, and Jesus answered.
A wicked man prayed, and Jesus answered.
A believing woman prayed, and Jesus answered.
All asked for something, and all got it.
Three very bad cases — devils, disease, death — beyond the reach of man (for man had tried and failed), cured by Christ.
Note the testimony of the evil spirit to Christ: saw Him afar off: ran and worshiped: confessed His divinity: dreaded His indignation.

2. Satan as a master is bad; his work worse; his wages worst of all.

19. A missionary convert.

22. It was his daughter's trouble that drove the ruler to Jesus.

5:23. "My daughter lieth at the point of death : I pray thee, come and lay thy hands on her that she may be healed: and she shall live." A short prayer, and to the point.

35. "Thy daughter is dead." A great part of the business of preachers to-day is to contradict this statement. Thy daughter, thy son, is *not* dead. Instead of ceasing to pray, be more urgent and earnest than ever.

6:20. "Herod feared John . . . and did many things." Had he feared God, he would have done everything.

Herod was once a hopeful case Mark 12:34. but the sin of adultery kept him back. It was the price of his soul.

27. John the Baptist, the last of the prophets, died as a martyr for the law of Moses, not because of his testimony concerning the Messiah.

31. "Come ye yourselves apart into a desert place, and rest awhile." There is progress in a Christian's life when he may not seem to be going ahead. Like a canal-boat in a lock, when it stands still but is rising all the time.

34. God the Father, "full of compassion." Ps. 145:8; 78:38. God the Son, "moved with compassion." Luke 7:13; Mark 1:41.

37. "Give ye them to eat." Christ uses us and our resources.

6 : 41. "Christ gave them to his disciples to set before them." Go and distribute.

7 : 24. "He could not be hid." As it is with the head, so it is with the members. Matt. 5 : 14.

   29. The Syrophœnician woman did what the lawyers and scribes could not do — she entangled Jesus.

8 : 34. You cannot follow *after* Jesus, until you have first come *to* him.

   36. He who sins for profit shall not profit by his sins.

   38. We are most ashamed of Jesus when He has most cause to be ashamed of us.

9 : 8. Jesus only. }
   34. Man only.

Jesus alone on the mount of transfiguration, and alone on the mount of suffering.

The Christian Life: —

"On the mountain-top" (v. 2).   "In the plain" (v. 9).
  Spiritual.   Practical.
  Communion.   Conflict.
  Occupied with Jesus.   Occupied for Jesus.

Jesus Only.

Once it was the blessing — now it is the Lord :
Once it was the feeling — now it is His word ;
Once His gifts I wanted — now Himself alone :
Once I sought for healing — now the Healer own :
Once 't was painful trying — now 't is perfect trust :
Once a half salvation — now the uttermost :

Once 't was what I wanted — now what Jesus says:
Once 't was constant asking — now 't is ceaseless praise,
Once it was my working — His it hence shall be:
Once I tried to use Him — now He uses me;
Once the power I wanted — now the Mighty One:
Once I worked for glory — now His will be done!

9 : 20. Like a bad tenant, the devil tried to do as much harm as he could when he got notice to quit.

10 : 17. Salvation sought and missed.

10 : 21. Jesus's first look was one of love: "Jesus beholding him loved him." V. 21.

Jesus's second look was one of sorrow: "Jesus looked round about," and said, "How hardly shall they that have riches enter into the kingdom of God." V. 23.

Jesus's third look was one of hope: "Jesus looking upon them saith, With men it is impossible, but not with God: for with God all things are possible." V. 27.

"One thing thou lackest" One leak can sink a ship, one sin destroy the sinner.

22. Men read the Old Testament story of earthly prosperity held out as a reward for well-doing, and the New Testament disclosure of heavenly joys beyond the highest earthly possessions, and they say they would like to have the Old Testament rewards in this world, and the New Testament treasures for the next world. The call of the Master comes in to decide for one or the other: not both.

10 . 33. Jesus proclaimed his coming sacrifice; hence He did not die a mere martyr's death.

    45. Jesus gave His life a ransom for many.
Jesus gave Himself for the church. Eph. 5:25.
Jesus gave Himself for me. Gal. 2:20.

13 : 36. A watchman on a boat was asked what he did when he felt sleepy. "I clean the lamp," he replied.

14 : 9. It is God's way, to magnify any good point He sees in us. Love hides sin.

15 : 21. Rutherford speaks of the sweet burdensomeness of Christ's cross. It is such a burden as wings to a bird or sails to a ship — it carries one forward to the desired haven.

LUKE.

1 : 20. That is why we have so many dumb Christians nowadays; they are waiting for tokens.

    26. Christ was foretold to: —
Adam — as a man. Gen. 3: 15.
Abraham — as to His nation. Gen. 22:18.
Jacob — as to His tribe. Gen. 49:10.
Isaiah — as to His family. Isa. 11:1-5.
Micah — as to His town. Micah 5:2.
Daniel — as to His time. Dan. 9:25.
Mary — as to His person. Luke 1:30.
By angels — as to His date. Luke 2:11.
By a star — as to His birthplace. Matt. 2:9.

LUKE. 119

1: 33. Napoleon established a kingdom by force, and it melted away. Jesus by love, and it keeps on spreading.

42. Infidelity has no songs. V. 46.

53. Christ sends none empty away but those who are full of themselves.

2: 1. When the time came for the prophecy regarding Christ's birth to be fulfilled, God put the whole world in motion to bring Mary to Bethlehem.

7. Jesus was born in a common house of entertainment where all might come to Him, and He died with His arms extended to receive all.

9. When Christ was born, midnight gloom lightened into midday brightness. When Christ died, midday darkened into midnight. See Luke 23:44.

10. God's covenant of works was for the Jewish people alone, but the glad tidings are for all people. Mark 16:15.

The angel — the first evangelist.

Contrast the giving of the Law (Ex. 19) with the dawn of the day of Grace.

14. Heaven's choir came down to sing when Heaven's King came down to save.

15. "Go and see"— a sure cure for doubt.

17. The first preachers of Christ.

25. "They also serve who only stand and wait."

2 : 49. "How is it that ye sought me? wist ye not that I must be about my Father's business?" The first recorded utterance of Jesus. His last: "It is finished." John 19 : 30.

4 : After Jesus had seen the open heavens, Satan tempted him. The more the blessing, the keener the temptation, for you are worth tempting.

3. Beware of the "if's" of the devil.

7. The price was too low. Christ was about to pay His life-blood for the Church, which is therefore safe until a higher price is offered.

11. A little danger but a great providence. "In their hands shall they bear thee up, lest at any time thou dash thy foot against a stone."

5 : 4. Trust God in the dark. Peter was an experienced fisherman and knew the best fishing grounds: yet he obeyed Christ, and with good result.

5. The Christian Church everywhere is "toiling," instead of seeking power from on high.

30. More persons are ready to shrink from sinners, than are ready to shrink from sin.

6 : 20. If you live by the gospel precepts, you may live on the gospel promises.
This life is all the heaven the worldling has, and all the hell the saint ever sees.
A Christian may be contented with his lot to-day, but not satisfied.

26. Said Socrates: "What evil have I done that this bad man commends me?"

6 : 31. Socialists have much to say on the golden rule, but they make two mistakes: —
- (1.) They make it apply to others more than to themselves, thus making it selfish.
- (2.) They urge the rule without the only true motive — a Christian one.

38 *Heaven's measure* — good measure — pressed down — shaken together — running over.

40. The Septuagint reads, "A scholar is not above his teacher, but everyone will be instructed as his teacher is." Not sinlessness, but "rounded to fulness."

45. "Would'st thou have me see thee?" said Socrates, "then speak; for speech reveals the man."

7 : 13. The widow of Nain was the saddest woman in all the city until she met Jesus.

27. Had the Messiah meant to appear as a temporal prince, his messenger would have appeared either in the pomp of a general or in the gaiety of a herald.

8 : 4. "The parable of the four kinds of soil"— the individual reception of the truth:—
- *a.* The wayside — Satan's thoroughfare (Matt. 19 : 8; Heb. 3 : 13); Pharaoh, Festus.
- *b.* Rocky — shallow and impulsive (Eze. 11 : 19; Gal. 5 : 7); Saul.
- *c.* Thorny — worldly (Gen. 3 : 18); Balaam, Judas, Ananias.
- *d.* Good.

Showing —
  a. Their deficiencies, dangers, possibilities.
  b. Quick response, exposure, early failure.
  c. Good seed, ready response, evil surroundings, disastrous development.
  d. Proper reception, healthy growth, rich harvesting.

One seed — four kinds of soil.

Three failures and one success! But the wayside may be broken up; the rocky ground blasted, the thorns uprooted.

10. "Unto you it is given to know the mysteries . . . but to others in parables." Just as the pillar of fire was seen by the Israelites, but to others it was a pillar of cloud.

12. Satan's punctuality, power, and purpose.

13. If sinners take up religion in a fair day, they will lay it down in a foul day. They are willing to go to sea, but on condition there are no storms. They think too much of wearing a thorn, though it is borrowed from Christ's crown.

9 : Notice seven points of weakness:—
  V. 10. The apostles told Jesus "all that *they* had done."
  V. 12. They said, "Send the multitude away."
  V. 32. "Peter and they that were with him were heavy with sleep."
  V. 40. They could not cast out the evil spirit.
  V. 46. They reasoned among them which should be greatest.

V. 49. They forbade another casting out devils.

V. 54. James and John asked Jesus to command fire from heaven and consume the Samaritans.

Man's thoughts are not as God's thoughts:—

Jesus said, "Give ye them to eat." The disciples replied that they had not enough.

Peter said, "It is good for us to be here." But while he spake, a cloud overshadowed them.

The disciples reasoned which of them should be greatest. Jesus, perceiving the thought of their heart, rebuked them.

They forbade another casting out devils. Jesus said, "Forbid him not."

They ask Jesus to command fire from heaven. He turned and rebuked them.

The man said, "Lord, suffer me first to go and bury my father." Jesus said, "Let the dead bury their dead."

10. The disciples told what *they* had done. Paul told what *God* had done. Acts 14: 27.

29. "As he prayed the fashion of his countenance was altered." It was prayer that brought out the inner man.

Growth in love tends to growth in loveliness Many a homely face is beautified by religion.

30. The churches become one on the Mount of Transfiguration.

Jesus the King.

Moses the lawgiver.

Elijah the prophet.

9 : 31. "Who spake of his decease which he should accomplish at Jerusalem." The shadow of the cross appears on the Mount of Transfiguration. Men talk of what interests them most. The death of Christ was the theme of conversation here.

33. It was good for Peter and James and John to be there, but not good to remain there.

59. No one who does not put Christ first is one of His. Would you rather work with a sexton's shovel or with a resurrection trumpet?

61. The greatest step to heaven is out of our own doors.

10 : 21. The only time it is recorded that Jesus rejoiced— "Because thou hast hid these things from the wise and prudent, and hast revealed them unto babes."

22. "No man knoweth who the Father is but the Son, and he to whom the Son will reveal him." Worship which is not *through Christ* is of an unknown God. John 14 : 6.

27. "Thou shalt love the Lord thy God . . . *and* thy neighbor as thyself." What God has joined, let not man put asunder.

28. The lawyer lacked, not knowledge, but the willingness to do what he knew to be his duty.
The priest and the Levite came "by chance;" not so the good Samaritan.
The Law never steps aside from its course.

10 : 40. "Dost thou not care?" These words were used by His disciples on another occasion, in tones almost blasphemous. Mark 4 : 38.

42. "One thing is needful"— the gospel.
"One thing I know." John 9 : 25.
"One thing have I desired." Ps. 27 : 4.
"One thing I do." Phil. 3 : 13, 14.
"Not one thing hath failed." Josh. 23 : 14.
"Be not ignorant of this one thing." 2 Peter 3 : 8.
"One thing thou lackest." Mark 10 : 21.

11 : 1. Pray, as a rest after service; as a preparation for important steps; as the condition of receiving the Spirit of God; as a preparation for sorrow. Pray in faith — reverence — humility — fervor — simplicity.

10. We ask for what we wish; we seek for what we miss; we knock for that from which we are shut out.

12 : 13. Even under Christ there were inattentive listeners.

15. A double caution against greed. Whenever Jesus spoke of wealth, he spoke in words of warning.

16. The anathema of the rich fool is not against riches, but against selfishness; against the mammon-worship which dethrones Jehovah.
Notice in this parable,—
   a. The false conception of life.
   b. Forgetfulness of divine providence.
   c. Denial of man's stewardship.

        d. Neglect of true self-providence, laying up treasure in heaven.

12 : 20. "Thou fool!" God's epitaph over this man. The world would have said, — "Here lies so-and-so, a good man, kind to the poor," etc.

       Why a fool? Because he thought he could fill his soul with the food his body enjoyed. The soul cannot eat and drink like the body. His soul was pining and starving in spiritual penury.

    37. "Blessed are those servants, whom the lord when he cometh shall find *watching*."

"Watching" — conduct governed by the constant expectation of the Lord's return. Vs. 42, 43.

    43. "Blessed is that servant, whom his lord when he cometh shall find so *doing*."

14 : 11. Where humility is the corner-stone, glory shall be the top-stone.

       V. 17. "Say to them that were bidden, *Come.*"
       V. 21. "*Bring in* hither the poor," etc.
       V. 23. "*Compel* them to come in."

    23. Religion a banquet.

Sometimes by theological wisdom, by church architecture, by our conduct, *we* compel people to stay away from the feast!

15 :   First parable — one lost in one hundred;
       Second parable — one lost in ten;
       Third parable — one lost in two.

       First parable — Christ seeking the sheep;
       Second parable — the Holy Spirit seeking the lost

sinner: inside "the house" (v. 8), that is, the church;

Third parable — the Father receiving the returning prodigal.

15: 2. "This man" — human, yet divine.

"Receiveth sinners" — His mission, the mark by which His enemies distinguished Him.

11. Contrast the story of Joseph and his father with that of the prodigal son and his father.

12. This young man had a fortune in his hand — not in his head or heart. Any fool can squander the former kind of fortune: but not the latter.

13. The farthest a Christian can get from heaven, is the world.

14–16. The devil has never had a famine of husks. There are always plenty of husks, and plenty of swine to eat them.

17. The prodigal might have said his father was the richest man in Judea, but no one would have believed him. The testimony of many Christians is not accepted by the world because of their spiritual poverty.

20. God was *in a hurry* to welcome the returning prodigal.

Eyes, heart, feet, hands, and lips — all engaged to welcome the wanderer.

The father saw him, had compassion, ran to him, embraced him, kissed him, clothed him, feasted him, rejoiced with him.

The backslider was missed from the family circle.

15 : 22. Robe of righteousness.
Ring of assurance.
Shoes of peace. Eph. 6 : 15.
{ Under the Law, God said, "Put off thy shoes." Ex. 3 : 5.
Under Grace, "Put on him the best robe." V. 22.

24. A sort of revival to which the elder brother objected.

29. No enjoyment with his father; only with his friends.
Six things about the prodigal son : —
His condition — "in want." V. 14.
His conviction — "came to himself." V. 17.
His confidence — "I will arise." V. 18.
His confession — "I have sinned." V. 18.
His contrition — "no more worthy." V. 19
His conversion — "He arose and came." V. 20.
Turning-points in his life : —
Sick of home. Vs. 12, 13.
Homesick. Vs. 17–19.
Home. Vs. 20–24.
Sequel. Vs. 25–32.
Six cases of men "afar off" from God:—
The prodigal. Chap. 15 : 13.
The rich man. Chap. 16 : 23.
The ten lepers. Chap. 17 : 12.
The publican. Chap. 18 : 13.
The beggar. Chap. 18 : 40.
Peter. Chap. 22 : 54.

16 : 20. In only one parable did Jesus use a proper name — Lazarus. In only four miracles do we know

LUKE. 129

the names of those benefitted — Mary Magdalene, Jairus, Malchus, Bartimæus.

When you step out of your self-contained residence, be sure you do not stumble over some Lazarus into hell.

22. You must not expect to toil for the prince of darkness all your life, and then to sup with the Prince of Light at the evening of death. You cannot go from Delilah's lap to Abraham's bosom.

24. It is better to beg bread on earth (as Lazarus) than water in hell (as Dives).

17 : 11-19. *Leprosy* is inherited; so is *Sin:* Rom. 5 : 19;
        contagious, Gen. 6 : 12;
        loathsome, Is. 1 : 6;
        fatal, James 1 : 15;
        separates its victim from his fellows, Eph. 2 : 17;
        healed through faith in Jesus, Eph. 2 : 8.

18 : 12. "I give tithes of all that I possess." Some people pride themselves on going by the Jewish rule, and giving one tenth. Go by the New Testament rule — give all you have.

People are supposed to contribute "according to their means," which often signifies "according to their meanness."

The Christian abuses the Jew for his stinginess, and yet is meaner than the Jew in his gifts to God.

18 : 30. I thank God I am not to have all my good things in this life; for then I should have nothing to anticipate in glory: and I thank God I am not to have all my good things in the life to come; for then I should have nothing to enjoy now.

19 : 4. The tree of Curiosity.
Curiosity led Eve to destruction; Zacchæus to salvation.

5. Jesus and Zacchæus met at the foot of the tree, and they have never parted since.

6. Curiosity took Zacchæus up the tree, but Love brought him down.

7. If Christ had declined to associate with sinners, He would have had a lonely time on earth.

9. Notwithstanding his bad reputation, there were streaks of good about Zacchæus, as there are about nearly every man. Gold is found in quartz, but sometimes in very small percentage.

10. In all heathen religions, man tries to find his gods, but in the Christian religion, God tries to find man.

21 : 8. Be not deceived.

9. Be not terrified.

14. Be not anxious.

34. Be not taken unawares.

22 : *Downward steps in Peter's path.*
Sleeping V. 45.

Smiting. V. 50.
Following afar off. V. 54.
Sitting among Christ's persecutors. V. 55.
Denying Christ. Vs. 57, 58, 60.
Contraries (Gal. 5 : 17) : —
Christ praying ; Peter sleeping.
" submitting ; Peter fighting.
" suffering like a lamb ; Peter cursing and swearing. Matt. 26 : 74.
Agents of Satan : —
Greed. V. 5.
Jealousy. V. 24.
Strife. V. 24.
Self-confidence. V. 33.
Temptation. V. 40.
Not watching. V. 46.
Lies. V. 57.

22 : 61, 62. One look from Christ undid all the devil's work.

23 : 12. There are sects and classes among the heathen, but they unite against Christianity.

32. Three crosses. Christ died *for* sin ; one man died *in* sin ; the other a sinner, but he died in faith.

38. Greek — the language of literature and art.
Latin — the language of power and conquest.
Hebrew — the language of religion.

42. The thief wanted to be remembered in heaven : Christ wanted to be remembered on earth.

42, 43. One repentance at death that none may despair; only one that none may presume.

The dying thief believed on Jesus at His worst.
From the side of Jesus Christ one man may go to heaven, another to hell.
Sin is either finished on Christ's cross, or forever confirmed upon the sinner's head.

23 : 43. Bossuet says,—
"' To-day '— what promptitude !
' With me '— what company !
' In Paradise '— what repose."

Prayer.   *Answer.*
Lord, remember me ..... Thou shalt be with me
when thou comest .... to-day
into thy kingdom ...... in Paradise.

24 : 3. As the grave of Jesus is empty, so shall all graves one day be.

   10. Women were the first evangelists of the resurrection.

   29. A three-fold blessing.
The presence of Jesus.   Ask for it.   V. 29.
The peace of Jesus.   Receive it.   V. 36.
Power from Jesus.   Wait for it.   V. 49.

JOHN.

In the gospel of John, the believer receives eight gifts :—
"The true bread."   Chap. 6 : 51.
"Eternal life."   17 : 2.
"Another comforter."   14 : 16.
"Peace."   14 : 27.

JOHN.

"The words that Thou gavest me." Chap. 17 : 8.
"A new commandment." 13 : 34.
"The glory which Thou gavest me." 17 : 22.
"Thy word." 17 : 14.

God's necessity — "Even so *must* the Son of man be lifted up." 3 : 14.

Man's necessity — "Ye *must* be born again." 3 : 7.

Christ's necessity — "He *must* increase." 3 : 30.

The servant's necessity — "I *must* decrease." 3 : 30.

The saint's necessity — "They that worship Him *must* worship Him in spirit and in truth." 4 : 24.

1 : The Trinity is inferred from three expressions in this chapter: —
    (1.) "In the bosom of the Father." V. 18.
    (2.) "The Lamb of God." V. 29.
    (3.) "The Spirit descending from heaven." V. 32.

"The word was God." V. 1.

"The Word was made flesh and dwelt among us." V. 14.

Jesus Christ was the Word, the living embodiment of the "first and great commandment,"—"Thou shalt love the Lord thy God . . . and thy neighbor as thyself." Matt. 22 : 37, 39.

1. God heard — the Word.
4. God felt — the life.
5. God seen — the light.

29. On the first day John led no one to Christ; on the second day, two. Vs. 35, 37.

The sin of the world took Jesus away, but at the same time He took the power of sin away.

1 : 31. Historical manifestation of Christ.
Spiritual   "   "   "   Chap. 2 : 11.
Resurrection "   "   "   Chap. 21 : 14.

37. John died young, but he led Andrew to Christ, and Andrew led Peter, and so the river flowed on.

38. Christ's first words to his disciples, "What seek ye?"
His last words, "Follow me." John 21 : 19, 22.

41. Christ laid the foundation of his Church on brotherly love, as he had also done in the Old Testament, beginning that earlier building on Moses and Aaron, who were brothers.

2 : 1–11. At the beginning and end of Christ's ministry, there were feasts in which wine was prominent.
Under the new dispensation the blood of the grape symbolizes the blood of the Paschal Lamb. Water is the type of death and sorrow; wine of joy. This miracle showed the character of Christ's ministry.

4. Mine "hour"— always "of death."
John 7 : 30.
    8 : 20.
   12 : 23.
   12 : 27.
   13 : 1.
   17 : 1.

2: 3. It is good to run short that we may be driven to Christ with our necessity.

10. Sin gives its best first — pleasures and honors. Its worst follows — sorrow, poverty, disgrace, ruin. First harlots and riotous living, then swine. First Goshen, then Egypt.

Christ gives first the cross, the race, the battle; then the crown, rest, and glory.

2: 11. Beginning of signs. Miracles are signs:—
- (1.) Of His divinity.
- (2.) Of His mission as from God.
- (3.) Of His good will toward men.
- (4.) Of the truth He taught.

Miracles did *not* manifest the glory of prophets or disciples.

3: 3. Regeneration — not imitation. }
Conversion — not evolution. }

Born once, die twice. }
Born twice, die once. }

It is remarkable that Christ declares the need of an entire change of heart and nature to a man of the highest honor, an eminent teacher, and a sincere inquirer; while He speaks the sublime truth, "God is a spirit," to an ignorant and abandoned woman. John 4: 24.

Had Nicodemus received light in abundance, he would not have stayed three years in the Sanhedrim, listening to all the cutting remarks he must have heard about Jesus.

His birth is truly low who is not born from above!
It were better to have no being than not to have
the "new being."

There are no still-born children in the family of
grace.

3: 4. An old sinner is nearer to the second death than
the second birth. It is hard to cast off the
devil's yoke when we have worn it long upon our
necks.

14. The brazen serpent was like the poisonous serpent,
yet without sting. So Christ was like man, but
without sin.

Only one way of healing for the dying Israelite —
not criticism, not philosophy, but obedience:
"Look!"

16. God's first covenant had been —
(1.) With a person, in Abraham.
(2.) Then with a family, in Jacob.
(3.) Then with a nation, in the people of Israel
at Sinai; and
(4.) Finally with "the world," embracing all the
other three, in Christ.

In creation, God gave the product of the earth for
our bodies. In redemption, He gave His only-
begotten Son for our souls.

4: Woman — Well — Worship — Witness — White
fields.

10. This woman was not interested in the gospel, but
she was interested in the water business; so
Christ spoke to her about that.

Twice on earth our Lord asked a favor and twice was he refused:—
  (1.) Here, when He asked for a drink.
  (2.) On the cross, when He asked for water, they gave Him vinegar. John 19: 28, 29.

4:14. God does not want a dam, but a canal to carry the gospel. Dam up a spring and you get a frog-pond.

Water rises to its level, and the water of life that comes from the throne of God will carry one into the presence of God.

15. She asked in ignorance, and He met her in mercy.

37. Any farm-laborer is called to reap, but it takes a skilful man to sow.

5:24. The voice of autumn is "from life unto death."

The voice of spring is "from death unto life."

35. John the Baptist was a "burning and a shining light." To burn is not enough—a firebrand does that. To shine is not enough—a glow-worm does that.

40. If youth be sick of the will-nots, old age is in danger of dying of the shall-nots.

6: *Seven classes of people in chapter 6 :—*
  1. Curious. V. 2.
  2. Admiring. V. 14.
  3. Greedy. V. 26.
  4. Skeptical. V. 36.
  5. Murmurers. V. 41.

6. Scoffers.   V. 52.
7. Backsliders.   V. 66.

6 : 27. A double paradox: —
(1.) Jesus tells them to work not for the perishable food, which they could only get by work:
(2.) But for the heavenly food, which they could only get by faith.

30. They wanted to see first, then to believe. This is inverting God's order.

35. Bread — the commonest article of food on our tables — is a type of Christ. It was through eating that Eve died. It is through eating that we may live.

8 : 12. It was "early in the morning" (v. 2), when Jesus shone into this poor woman's heart. Then, possibly, looking out on the early sun, He said, "I am the light of the world."

9 : 1. Jesus hid himself from people with sight, but revealed himself to people without sight.

4. It is lamentable that we should live so long a time in the world and do so little for God : and that we should live so short a time in the world and do so much for Satan.

5. Hume said to a minister, the light of nature was all he wanted. On going down stairs, Hume declined a light because the moon was high enough, and as he said it, he tumbled down stairs.

9 : 6. John McNeill says the blind man was made out of clay, so clay was a good thing to mend him with.

These means seem eccentric. Such is the gospel in the opinion of the worldly wise. They sneer at "the blood," and cry for "culture," "education."

20. Christ opened the eyes of a blind man and he saw his father. You can open a man's eyes so that he shall see God.

27. Trying to make converts already.

10 : 9. Safety — liberty — nourishment.

14. "I am the Good Shepherd."
John calls Jesus the Good Shepherd because He laid down His life for the sheep.

Paul calls Jesus the Great Shepherd because He rose from the dead. Heb. 13 : 20.

Peter calls Jesus the Chief Shepherd because He is coming again. 1 Peter 5 : 4.

27. Christ's sheep have two marks: —
(1.) In their ears, "They hear my voice;"
(2.) In their feet, "They follow me."

A sick sheep will not follow the shepherd.

37. "If I do not the works of my Father, believe me not." That is, if I live contrary to the life of a Christian, do not take me for a Christian.

11: *Lazarus*, a type of the sinner, as to being —
  (1.) dead ;
  (2.) raised up ;
  (3.) seated ;
  (4.) feasting ;
  (5.) testifying.

The miracle of raising Lazarus from the dead is a parable of spiritual life.

25. A man was conversing with a high Brahmin priest who could not see the divinity of Jesus, and he asked : "Could *you* say, 'I am the resurrection and the life'?" "Yes," he answered, "I could say that." "*But could you make any one believe it ?*"

35. Pagan deities wept and bellowed when wounded, but were never touched with the feeling of human infirmities.

43. It was a good thing Jesus called Lazarus by name, otherwise every dead man in the graveyard would have come forth.

12 : 20–24. Jesus talked of *death* to the Greeks who all the time dwelt on the beautiful, etc. See 1 Cor. 1 : 22.

You can never cultivate self into anything but self.

Jesus died alone : but three thousand at Pentecost were the harvest of His death.

13 : 5. You may wash the saints' feet, but not with scalding water.

13:17. To obey the truth and not know it, is impossible. To know the truth and not obey it, is unprofitable.

Divine knowledge is not as the light of the moon, to sleep by, but as the light of the sun, to work by.

14: 2. Those who look for a heaven made ready will live as though they were already in heaven.

20. "Ye in me"— The believer's standing.
"I in you" — The believer's strength.

23. Faith makes all things possible;
Love makes all things easy.

27. To fear is to have more faith in your antagonist than in Christ. What we get from God, we cannot keep without God.

15: 2. *a.* No fruit. V. 2.
b. Fruit. V. 2.
c. More fruit, due to the purging. V. 2.
d. Much fruit, due to the abiding. Vs. 5, 8.

5, 8, etc. The root can only show its strength and glory in the branches. Fruitful branches bend low.

God has made no provision in the Bible for isolation. Scripture expressions all show a contrary state of things : —
We are "branches" in the vine,
"members" in the body,
"stones" in the temple,
"brothers and sisters" in the family,

bearing a close relation to each other. We have first to look up and realize our relation to God; and then to learn the various relationships we have to our neighbors. All are in their different niches, filling the place God has given them; and we must desire, not only to serve God, but by love to serve one another.

15 : 15. If we lived nearer heaven we should have earlier notice of God's purposes.

16. "Ye have not chosen me, but I have chosen you." I do not know one passage in the Bible where choice is connected with salvation.

20. A general was leading his army to battle. His men asked what he would give them. "Hunger, cold, wounds, and death." They were silent for a time, then threw up their hands and said, "We will go."

16: 2. Six men were turned out of Oxford for praying. Among them were the two Wesleys and Whitfield.

8–11. The *Holy Spirit in relation to the world.* Convicting —
   a. Of Christ crucified — sin.
   b. Of Christ glorified
   c. Of Christ to come — Judgment.

10. What is the meaning of "and ye see me no more"? *Ans.*—When the high priest went into the Holiest of Holies, the people knew they were accepted by God when he returned. But Christ went

away. So He sent the Holy Spirit to assure us of our acceptance.

Conscience convicts of —
Sin committed.
Righteousness impossible.
Judgment to come.

The Holy Spirit convicts of —
Sin committed.
Righteousness imputed.
Judgment past.

The former is legal, the latter gospel.

16:12. Much of the truth that the Bible contains is written in sympathetic ink, invisible until the time is ripe.

17:15. The true conception of "separation"—"I pray not that thou shouldest take them out of the world, but that thou shouldest keep them from the evil."

18:10. Peter's rashness in smiting the man helped to identify him, and led to his denial of Christ. Vs. 26, 27.

38. Here is a curious anagram on Pilate's question, "What is truth?" In Latin this is "*Quid est veritas?*" The letters can be arranged so as to read, "*Est vir, qui adest,*" meaning, "It is the man who is before you."

39. Did Nicodemus remember that evening when he heard Christ say, "The Son of man must be lifted up"?

20 : 17. "Touch me not." Was Christ thinking of the ritual (see Lev. 7 : 19)?

28. Thomas was an honest doubter. He did not accept Christ's offer to feel the nail-prints. Faith is not to be obtained at your fingers' ends.

21 : 6. Jesus was the secret of their success.

11. "Great fishes, an hundred and fifty and three." One evidence that John wrote this epistle. Who but a fisherman would have counted the fish, and told how big they were?

15. The greatest example of faith we know is that of Jesus going away and not calling legions of angels to spread the gospel, but leaving it to Peter and the others.

At first the shepherds used to feed the sheep; but when corruption crept in, the sheep had to feed the shepherds.

An old writer said that in the early days the Church had wooden chalices and golden bishops, but now we have wooden bishops and golden chalices.

ACTS.

The acts of the Holy Spirit.

1 : 4. "Wait for the promise of the Father." Tarry at a promise till God meets you there. He always returns by the way of His promises.

The promises of God are the moulds into which we pour our prayers.

1·11. "In like manner." Hence we may expect that Jesus will come —
  (1.) Personally.
  (2.) Visibly.
  (3.) In the clouds.

2 : 1. Pentecost was the birthday of the Holy Spirit whose dispensation will close at Christ's second coming. The Holy Spirit was present before, but not incarnate in the Church, just as Christ was ever present, but not incarnate.

3. "Fire." Fill the cup with incense, and load the altar with odorous wood, but fire is still needed to send out fragrance. So the preacher's talent, genius, and other gifts need fire from above, before they can achieve results.

8. When God set forth his fiery law (Deut. 33 : 2), He proclaimed it in *one* tongue; but the story of grace was told in the language of every nation under heaven.

21. "Whosoever shall call on the name of the Lord shall be saved." It is remarkable that though more than a million Jews perished during the siege of Jerusalem, no Christians perished, for they withdrew to Pella, on the approach of the Roman army.

23. The Jews nailed Jesus on the cross and so sent Him to heaven, and now they go about the streets selling old clothes.

2 : 37. Threefold result of being filled with the Spirit: —
Pricked in their heart. Acts 2 : 37.
Cut to the heart. 7 : 54.
Turned the world upside down. 17 : 6.

41. The first time the law was preached three thousand were killed. Ex. 32 : 28. The first time grace was preached three thousand were saved.

47. "Added to the Church." See Acts 5 : 14, 11 : 24. "Added to the Lord," because the Church is the body of Christ.

3 : 2. Almost all the alms of the world are administered at the gates of the temple, by them that go up to the temple at the hour of prayer.

21. "The times of restitution of all things."

The earth restored to man by re-genesis.

The body " " the soul by resurrection

The soul " " God by regeneration.

4 : *The Name of Jesus:* —
V. 7. By what name have ye done this?
V. 10. By the name of Jesus Christ.
V. 12. "There is none other name under heaven given among men, whereby we must be saved."

31. Hugh Latimer was ordered by Henry VIII to apologize for a too plain sermon he preached. But he was sent by a higher King and *repeated* the **sermon.**

5 : 31. As a Prince, Jesus gives repentance,
As a Saviour, He gives remission of sins.

6 : 5. Six good things about Stephen —
(1.) Full of faith. V. 5.
(2.) " " the Holy Ghost. V. 5.
(3.) " " power. V. 8.
(4.) Full of irresistible wisdom and energy. V. 10.
(5.) Full of sunshine. V. 15.
(6.) An intrepid witness for God. Chap. 7.

15. Three men in the Bible whose faces shone: Moses, Jesus, and Stephen.

Dr. Bonar once said: "Did you ever notice, Brother Whittle, that when the Jews accused Stephen of blasphemous words against Moses (v. 11), the Lord lit up his face with the same glory with which Moses's face shone?"

7 : 2. Stephen only preached this one sermon that we know of, but out of his death came Paul, the greatest preacher since Christ.

23–36. Eighty years of training for forty years of service.

50. There are few death-bed scenes in the Bible.

7 : 60. } Augustine says the Church owes Paul to the pray-
8 : 1 } ers of Stephen.

27. The story of a man who was wrong and knew it; who was set right, and gave evidence of being right (vs. 36, 39, rejoicing).

9 : 3. Four recorded visions to Paul: —
    (1.) For his conversion. Acts 9 . 3, 4.
    (2.) For his work. Acts 16 · 9.
    (3.) For his strengthening. Acts 18 : 9.
    (4.) For his preservation. Acts 27 · 23, 24.

11 : 1. Israel is God's first-born, but the Gentiles are his second-born.

    26. "Called Christians." Not in derision, but by God's providence. The Church is Christ's body, and the body of a man goes by the same name as the head. Col. 1 . 18, 24.

    A dead church is like a dwarf with fine, large head but crippled body.

15 : 11. Saved by grace. Acts 15 : 11.

    Stand in grace. Rom. 5 : 2.

    Grow in grace. 2 Peter 3 : 18.

16 : 9. Dr Bonar used to say that the "man of Macedonia" turned out to be a woman ; see v. 15.

    Suppose Paul and Silas had been ordered east instead of west, these lands of ours would have been what India and Africa now are, and missionaries from there would be bringing us the gospel.

    13. Paul was not a man who was a devout worshiper in Jerusalem, but who, when he came to Philippi, spent his Sabbaths as the Philippians did. Out of Paul's steady-going habits came this story of grace and salvation.

16 : 14. Attention, humanly speaking, is the avenue by which the Lord Jesus enters into the soul. If you had listened with attention and intention for five minutes to the poorest preacher you ever heard, you would have been converted.

15. First the heart, then the home. "If ye have judged me to be faithful to the Lord, come into my house, and abide there."

31. Believing *on* Jesus or *in* Jesus is a great deal more than believing *about* Jesus.

17 : 22. Paul's sermon on Mars' Hill : —
God is Creator, Ruler (v. 24) ; independent (v. 25) ; approachable (v. 27) ; immanent (v. 28).
True worship (v. 25).
God's bounties to man (v. 25).
Gracious privilege or command (v. 27).
Wrong views of God (v. 29).
Repentance commanded (v. 30).
Universality of sin (v. 30).
Day of judgment (v. 31).

Idolatry is falsely directed worship, yet it bears witness to the ineradicable needs of humanity.

28. "For we are also His offspring." A poet's sentiment — a preacher's theme.

Men talk of "universal brotherhood" and reject the God and Father of us all.

30. The more a man is troubled about sin now, the less he will be troubled by sin hereafter.

17 : 31. The world is redeemed by believing on the Son of
man, and hereafter the world will be judged by
the Son of man.

> A sad conclusion : —
> Some mocked, v. 32 ,
> some procrastinated, v. 32 ;
> but some believed, v. 34

18 : 9. The Lord sees and knows you, especially if you are
weak and fainting.

19 : 18, 19. Fruits of the revival. "Many that believed came
and confessed and showed their deeds. Many of
them also which used curious arts brought their
books together and burned them before all men."

    25. Demetrius cried up the goddess Diana, but it was
her silver shrines, not her temple, he so much
adored.

20 :   Tears of personal suffering. V. 19.
       " " pastoral solicitude. V. 31.
       " " friendly sympathy. V. 37.

26 : 18 God first forgives; then He gives.

> A perfect man has three eyes: —
> 1. The eye of sense.
> 2 The eye of reason.
> 3. The eye of faith.
>
> Every animal has the first; every man has the second and third; but only the regenerate man uses the third to see the things of God.

The gospel gives sight, light, liberty, pardon, heaven.

The sinner is disinherited, but Christ restores him.

26 : 28. "Almost."

Almost hot is lukewarm. Rev. 3 : 16.

Almost a child is a bastard.

Almost sweet is unsavory.

28 : 30. The Bible has little to say about the endings of its heroes, but much about their beginnings. Cf. Moses, Paul, Peter. We know nothing of the end of Jeremiah, etc., etc.

ROMANS.

Paul was peculiarly fitted for a great work among the Gentiles: —
    1. By birth, a Hebrew.
    2. By citizenship, a Roman.
    3. By culture, a Greek.

Justified —
  By His grace. Chap. 3 : 24.
  By faith. 3 : 28; 5 : 1.
  By works. 4 : 2.
  By His blood. 5 : 9.

1 : 16. It is God's word, not our comment on it, that **saves** souls.

The glory of the gospel is that it comes to the unfit, to those who have thwarted and resisted

God. The survival of the fittest does not apply.

Justification means that God declares a man just by judicial act.

Righteousness means that God clothes him with His own righteousness which sanctifies as well as justifies.

2:16. God judges the world by the same rule that He has given the world to act by — Jesus Christ.

3:15. A French proverb says, "Evil comes on horseback and goes away on foot."

20. The law does not create nor remove, but simply reveals, the evil in man's heart: just as a plumbline. It does not alter or improve man's nature or impart power to meet its demands.

The law can pursue a man to Calvary, but no further.

5: Peace for the past. V. 1.

Grace for the present. V. 2.

Glory for the future. V. 2.

Much more being justified by his blood. V. 9.

Much more being reconciled. V. 10.

Much more the grace of God hath abounded. V. 15.

Much more they . . . shall reign. V. 17.

Much more grace did abound. V. 20.

5: 3 "Glory in tribulation." G-L-O-R-Y spells glory, not "growl."

  6. We were without strength, v. 6;
            ungodly, v. 6;
            sinners, v. 8,
            enemies, v. 10.

  12. Man renews his faculties every seven years. We cannot account for death except by sin.

Were it not for sin, death would never have had a beginning. Were it not for death, sin would never have an ending.

Sin debases a man in this life, and destroys him in the life to come

5 : 20. The law brings out sin ; Grace covers it. The law wounds ; the gospel heals. One is a quiver of arrows ; the other a cruise of oil.

6 :   Distinguish between —
     a. Our position — standing in God' sight.
     b. Our condition — experience in daily life.
     For *a*, look to the cross of Christ.
     For *b*, look to the Holy Spirit in you.

Justification is the work of Christ.

Sanctification is the work of the Holy Spirit.

  18. Such as have received Christ's bounty are unwilling to fight under Satan's banner

  23. "The wages of sin is death." The works of sin are dishonorable, but its wages are mortal.

7 : 5. The law proposes life as the end of obedience ; the gospel gives life as the only proper ground of obedience

The law demands strength from one who has none, and curses for failure.

The gospel gives strength to one who has none, and blesses him for using it.

There is no sin so little as not to kindle an eternal fire. Its first-born is death : its last last-born is hell.

11. "Sin deceived me" Deceitful, else never delightful. Deceitful as to the satisfaction to be found in it, the excuse to be made for it, and the probability of its punishment.

7 : 18. "Flesh." Drop the "h," as they are apt to do in London, spell backward, and you have "s e l f.'

21. We all carry around with us material that Satan can work upon.

24. "Who shall deliver me from the body of this death ?" Certain criminals used to be punished at that time by binding a corpse fast to them.

8 : This chapter begins with "no condemnation," and ends with "no separation."

Spurgeon called these glorious doctrines of chapter 8, "golden stepping-stones through the ' slough of despond.'"

8 : 3. God has sent his Son in the image of us all that He might make all of us sons in the image of that One.

9. You might as well try to hear without ears, or breathe without lungs, as try to live a Christian life without the Spirit of God in your heart.

The Indians refused to be baptized by the Spaniards, because they treated them so cruelly. "For," said they, "he must be a cruel God who has such servants."

17. Both beggar and heir.

23. The child of God may "groan," but never "grumble." He has no more right to grumble than to swear.

Holy Spirit for us.   V. 26.
God for us.   V. 31.
Christ for us.   V. 34.

29. "Called according to his purpose." My faith is the reflection of God's eternal purpose. We are *expected* when we come to Christ.

38. Paul's persuasions : —
No separation from the love of God (here).
Nothing unclean of itself. . . . Chap. 14 : 14.
He is able to keep. . . . 2 Tim. 1 : 12.

10 : 9. Unbelief. Christ may dwell in the heart where unbelief lurks, but not where it reigns.

10 : 17. Faith is the sacrifice of the understanding to God : repentance is the sacrifice of the will.

11 : 6. Works may be good crutches to go upon, but they are bad christs to lean upon.

Works magnify man, grace magnifies God. We had better let works go, and build alone upon free grace.

Good works may be our Jacob's staff — to walk with on earth ; but they never can be our Jacob's ladder to climb up to heaven.

17. Brands plucked from the fire (Zech. 3 : 2),
become branches (Rom. 11 : 17), and
bear much fruit (John 15 : 8).

20. The Jews broken off, because of unbelief.

The Gentiles grafted in, because of belief.

12 : 3. Humility is to have a just estimate of one's self.

10. "In honor preferring one another." Like the ancient Roman who said, "Thank God, Rome has better men than me," when another was elected to fill his office.

13. Many love at their tongue's end, but the godly love at their fingers' end.

13 : 9, 10. "Love is the fulfilling of the law."
1. Love to God will admit no other gods.
2. Love resents everything that debases its object by representing it by an image.

3 Love to God never will dishonor His name.
4. Love to God will reverence His day.
5. Love of parents makes one honor them.
6. Hate, not love, is a murderer.
7. Lust, not love, commits adultery.
8. Love will give, but never steal.
9. Love will not slander or lie.
10 Love's eye is not covetous.

14 : 21. The wicked stumble at every straw in the way to heaven, but they climb over hills in the way to destruction.

15 : 24. "Somewhat filled." Christ alone can fill.

I CORINTHIANS.

1 : 26. "Not many wise men after the flesh, not many mighty, not many noble, are called." Yet the Lord always has some wise, some mighty, some noble, among his disciples. Joseph of Arimathea was not called to be a fisherman.

Luther once said of a pious queen of Denmark, "Christ will sometimes carry a queen to heaven."

Rich men are choice dishes at God's table.

When the tutor of King James I. lay dying, his Majesty sent to enquire about him. "Tell my Sovereign," said the tutor, "that I am going where few kings go."

1 : 27, 28. God's five workers. —
1. Foolish things.
2. Weak things.
3. Base things.
4. Things which are despised.
5. Things which are not.

2 : 1–4. It is our duty to declare God's truth. It is the Spirit's office to demonstrate it.

Effort is ours.   Effect is his.

9, 10. The things revealed by the Spirit have not been perceived by the eye, received by the ear, or conceived by the heart of man.

11–13. The Spirit knows the things of God, makes us know God's gifts to us, and teaches us to speak of them to others.

14. All God's ways are foolishness to the worldly. But as old men say of the young, "They think us fools; we know them to be fools."

3 : 1. "Babes."
   (1.) Wheeled around by others — by every doctrine.
   (2.) Fed on milk, which has passed through the digestion of another — others' opinions.
   (3.) Not filled with the power of the Holy Spirit.

6. *Religion* is a plant that will die unless it is watered. *Ungodliness* is a weed which grows without planting, and which will not die without being plucked up.

3 : 8. God rewards according to the work done, not according to the harvest.

16. The Spirit of God is ejected to make room for other tenants whenever we fall into sin.

6 : 19. George Muller once said, "I cannot take care of my soul, God can keep that; but my body is for me to take care of."

A professor at Lafayette College, at the funeral of his son, said to the young men who bore the coffin, "Tread lightly, for you are bearing a temple of the Holy Ghost."

20. A girl told Luther that she had sold herself to the devil. He said she could not do so, for she was not her own.

8 : 13. Better deny yourself of anything than make your brother to offend.

9 : 16. Some preach all doctrine, for the head: that makes an imperfect man.
Some preach all experience, for the heart: that makes an imperfect man.
Some preach all works, for the hands: that makes an imperfect man.
Preach doctrine, experience, and works, and you get a perfect man.

22. Use bait that the fish like.

24. "So run, that ye may obtain." The high prize of heavenly bliss is at the end of the gospel race.

A crown for the runner; a curse for the runaway.

10 : 12. Not only the young go astray; e. g., Abram, Noah, Lot, David, Peter, etc.

13. To be tempted is not to sin. The strongest attacks are made on the strongest forts.

31. It was once said of a humble Christian man, "that his business was shoemaking." He happened to be present, and said, "Excuse me, my business is to glorify God. I earn my bread by making shoes."

12 : 4. "Now there are diversities of gifts, but the same Spirit." Union, not uniformity, among Christians.

13 : 2. Knowledge puffeth up. Love alone buildeth up.

4. Beware of envy Cain's envy hatched Abel's murder.

13 : 13. Faith ends in sight.
Hope ends in presence.
Charity — love — never ends.
Faith gets the most.
Humility keeps the most.
Love works the most.

14 : 9. H. L. Hastings was at a meeting and was called on to speak. He just said he had nothing to say. Some one else spoke, and souls were saved at that meeting.

15 : 9. Paul's experience : —
A. D. 59, "Least of the apostles." Rom 15 9.

A. D. 64, "Less than the least of all saints." Eph. 3 : 8.

A. D. 65, "Chief of sinners." 1 Tim. 1 : 15.

15 : 22. The first Adam was for self-advancement ; the second Adam for self-abasement. The former was for deifying self ; the latter, for crucifying flesh.

47. There are only two men in God's sight : one in Eden, the other on Golgotha.

53. "Corruptible," — referring to those who are dead at Christ's coming. "Mortal," referring to those who are then alive.

54. Death is but a physical, incident in an immortal career. It is a covenant blessing to the child of God, for "He giveth His beloved sleep."

56. A believer may feel the *stroke* of death, but he shall never feel the *sting* of death.

58. "*Always* abounding." Most Christians think it is enough to abound on Sundays.

II CORINTHIANS.

1 : 4. "*Tribulatio*" is a Roman threshing-instrument, used to separate the wheat from the chaff.

10. Deliverance, past, present, and future.

12. Conscience is the voice of the soul. The passions are the voice of the body.

Conscience is an anchor. Terrible it is, but true, that like the anchor, conscience may be carried away.

2 : 11. Gabriel gave Daniel "skill and understanding" in the time of his perplexity. Dan. 9 : 22.

3 : 3. We cannot all be "apostles," but we ought to be "epistles" — love-letters from Jesus to the world.

"Illuminated Texts."

16. Faith precedes enlightenment.

4 : 17. Afflictions are but the shadows of God's wings. The darker the night, the brighter the stars. The hotter the fire, the purer the gold.

5 :   V. 1. A new body, — resulting in —
Sanctification, v. 2;
Separation, v. 8;
Service, v. 9;
Suffering, v. 4;
Surrender, v. 4.
V. 7. A new walk.
V. 15. A new life.
V. 17. A new nature.
V. 18. A new attitude.
V. 21. A new standing.

2. Homesick for heaven. "We groan, earnestly desiring to be clothed upon with our house which is from heaven."

8. When an old martyr laid his head on the block, one said to him, "Shut thine eyes a little and thou shalt see God."

10. As you live, you'll die, and as you die, you'll live forever.

5 : 14. If the love of God sets us to work, the God of love will find us the wages.

20. "Now then, we are ambassadors for Christ." An ambassador —
(1) Is always sent to a foreign land,
(2) With which we are at peace.
(3) He has to go to that country, and not let them come to him.
(4) They judge of his country by his example.
(5) He has a message.

21. "He made him to be sin who knew no sin" — made to be *sin*, not a *sinner*.

6 : 4-10. Sevenfold passive suffering.
Sevenfold active self-denial.
Sevenfold means of enduring labor.
Sevenfold result.

10. Outward trouble — inward joy.
The backslider in heart, even amid outward joy, has inward sorrow. Prov. 14 : 13, 14.
Paul's testimony before the Church.

7 : 10. "For godly sorrow worketh repentance to salvation not to be repented of, but the sorrow of the world worketh death."
Godly sorrow (i. e., after the mind of God), is Godward and God-wrought.
Sorrow of the world is like Balaam's, when he said, "I have sinned," yet continued to sin.

9 : 7. "God loveth a cheerful giver." "I can give so much without feeling it." Is that right?

10 : 10. Love will stammer rather than be dumb

11 : 14. Satan fashioneth himself into —
    An angel of light. 2 Cor. 11 : 14.
    A roaring lion. 1 Peter 5 : 8.
    A beguiling serpent. Gen. 3 : 3.

12 : 7. God many times places a thorn in the flesh to prick the bladder of pride.

    There is no gathering a rose without a thorn, until we get to Beulah land.

  9. In the divine partnership we contribute weakness. With a loving acceptance of God's will comes peace.

13 : 5. Contemplation is a perspective-glass to see our Saviour in. Examination is a looking-glass to see ourselves by.

GALATIANS.

Five aspects of Crucifixion in Galatians: —
    I crucified in Christ. Chap. 2 : 20.
    Christ crucified for me. 3 : 1.
    The flesh crucified in me. 5 : 24.
    The world crucified unto me. 6 : 14.
    I crucified unto the world. 6 : 14.

1 : 16. Some one asked Roland Hill what he thought would become of the heathen. He said, "If I do n't see some of them in heaven, I 'll see the reason for it."

2 : 19. I, through the law's operations on Christ, am dead to the law's condemnation

2:20. "I was crucified," in Jesus on the cross.

There are two centers of being — the self-life, and the Christ-life.

3:13. Christ on the cross delivers from the penalty of sin.

Christ at God's right hand delivers from the power of sin.

Christ coming in the clouds delivers from the presence of sin.

4:16. Truth is not always relished where sin is nourished

18. Many a man can dance till six o'clock in the morning, but few Christians pray or preach so long.

5:11. The cross of Christ is an "offence". —

1. To morality; because works cannot justify.
2. To philosophy; because it appeals to faith, not reason.
3. To culture; because its truth is revealed to babes.
4. To caste; because God chooses the poor and humble.
5. To the will; because it calls for unconditional surrender.

V. 16. Walk in the Spirit.
V. 18. Be led of the Spirit.
V. 25. Live in the Spirit.

22. Three houses: No. 1, Love; No. 2, Joy; No. 3, Peace.

Three sisters that meet us at the threshold of God's kingdom· Love, Joy, Peace.

The fruits of the Spirit in terms of *love:* —
Joy is love exulting.
Peace is love reposing.
Longsuffering is love untiring.
Gentleness is love enduring.
Goodness is love in action.
Faith is love on the battlefield.
Meekness is love under discipline.
Temperance is love in training.

6 : 1. While we seek to heal a wound in our brother's actions, we should be careful not to leave a scar upon his person.

2. Miss Fidelia Fiske tells us that she was seated on a warm Sabbath afternoon on the earthen floor of her mission chapel, feeling quite exhausted. A Syrian woman came and sat behind her and said, "If you love me, lean hard."
A true Christian grows stronger by his loads.

7. The flower of life is planted by God. Shall it be plucked by the devil?

10. There is an inscription in Shrewsbury : —

"For our Lord Jesus Christ's sake,
Do all the good you can,
To all the people you can,
By all the means you can,
In all the places you can,
As long as ever you can."

"Lost! Somewhere between sunrise and sunset: Two golden hours, each set off with sixty diamond minutes. No reward offered, for they are lost forever."

Opportunity : —

    (1.) Swift in motion.
    (2.) Never returns.
    (3.) Must be improved while it is passing.

EPHESIANS.

Seven "walks" of Ephesians : —

2 : 2. "Trespasses and sins wherein in time past ye *walked*."
2 : 10. "Good works . . . we should *walk* in them."
4 : 1. "*Walk* worthy of the vocation wherewith ye are called"
4 : 17. "*Walk* not as other Gentiles walk."
5 : 2. "*Walk* in love."
5 : 8. "*Walk* as children of light."
5 : 15. "*Walk* circumspectly."

1 : 4. Do not stumble at the doctrine of election. Preach the gospel to all, and (as some one has said) if you convert any one who was not "chosen," God will forgive you.

22. While Christ, my Head, is in heaven, I am all right on earth.

The church is Christ's body. There is only one head ; hence don't speak about this body and that body of Christians.

2: 2. Those who once walked according to the prince of the power of the air are now built together into a habitation of God. V 22.

5. "Dead in sins" means dead in the senses by which we apprehend God.

7. Riches of His goodness (on earth) in trees, corn, etc.
Riches of His grace (from the cross).
Riches of His glory (upon the throne)

An old colored woman who was an earnest Christian, lay dying. Some one asked her why God would save an old sinner like her. She answered, "God is g'win to p'int the angels to me and tell 'em to see what the grace of God can do."

8. God works alone in creation, redemption, regeneration.

The best way to get to heaven is to take the oar of faith in one hand, and the oar of works in the other, and pull ahead.

10. "Created in Christ Jesus unto good works."

a. The starting-point — "Created in Christ Jesus."

Cursed in the first birth, but blessed in the second.

b. The path — good works its general characteristic.

The creature and the path both "prepared" (see margin), by God, hence make no complaint of your lot.

c. The pace — walk.

Saved "*through* faith . . . *unto* good works."

V. 19. The household of God.
V. 21. An holy temple in the Lord.
V. 22. An habitation of God.

3: 8. "The unsearchable riches of Christ." A Spanish ambassador once said to a French ambassador, "My master's treasure-house has no bottom," referring to the Mexican mines.

4: 4. The seven-twisted cord of Christian unity: "One body — one Spirit — one hope — one Lord — one faith — one baptism — one God and Father of all."

10. As the clouds carry rain, but not for themselves, so Christ carries grace for thee.

11. "Some evangelists; and some pastors and teachers."
Dead men need evangelists
Living men need pastors and teachers.
Evangelists — quarrymen who dig out the stone.
Pastors — stone squarers who take off the rough edges.
Teachers — masons who put them in place.

26. The way to "be angry and sin not," is to be angry as Christ was, at nothing but sin.

5: 14. "Awake, thou that sleepest, and arise from the dead, and Christ shall give thee light."
The sinner described.
The sinner addressed.
The sinner pointed to the Saviour.

5 : 18. "Be not drunk with wine, . . . but be filled with the Spirit"

Two commands, both equally binding

6 : 5-9. God has wedded labor and capital together; and what God has joined, let not demagogues tear asunder.

11. An old Hussite leader said to his soldiers, when about to die: "My enemies are afraid of me. Take my skin and make a drum-head of it, and they will still be afraid of me"

Bunyan remarks, "The Christian has no armor for his back."

"Able to stand against the wiles of the devil." 6 : 11.

"Able to withstand in the evil day." 6 : 13.

"Able to quench all the fiery darts of the wicked." 6 · 16.

18. Prayer must always be the fore-horse of the team. Do whatever is wise, but not till thou hast prayed. Send for the physician if thou art sick, but first pray. Begin, continue, and end everything with prayer.

PHILIPPIANS.

Trust in the Lord. Chap. 2 : 19, 24.
Rejoice in the Lord. 3 : 1; 4 : 4, 10.
Stand fast in the Lord. 4 : 1.
"The gospel" in Philippians:—
Fellowship in the gospel. 1 : 5.
Furtherance of the gospel. 1 : 12.

Defence of the gospel. 1.17.
Faith in the gospel. 1·27.
Service in the gospel. 2:22.
Laboring in the gospel 4.3.

1: 6. Mr. Spurgeon, leaning over the platform of a church where a work of grace was going on, heard a penitent below in great distress pray earnestly, "Lord, make a good job of me! Lord, make a good job of me!"

21. One of the old martyrs said to his persecutors as they were leading him to death: "You take a life from me that I cannot keep, and bestow a life upon me that I cannot lose."

2: 12. Paul tells Christians ("beloved"), to "work out" their salvation. Unless God has first worked it into you, you cannot work it out.

14. When a horse begins to kick, he stops pulling. Same way with church members.

Murmuring is quarreling with God.
Disputing is quarreling with men.
A murmur means, "I could have managed this thing better than God."

3: 9. That garment of righteousness which was worn to shreds on Adam's back will never make a covering for mine.

17. Cicero complained of Homer that he taught the gods to live like men. Grace teaches men to live like God.

4 : 1. An old man had gone to California to see his sons who had become rich. On being asked to go to the theater, he said he had traveled far, but not far enough to forget his principles.

6. Our great matters are little to His power : our little matters are great to His love.
Be careful for nothing.
Be prayerful for everything.
Be thankful for anything.
Let your riches consist, not in the largeness of your possessions, but in the fewness of your wants.

12. It is difficult to walk in the clear day of prosperity without wandering, or in the dark day of adversity without stumbling.

COLOSSIANS.

1 : 5. There is a "heavenly hope" laid up for the youngest believer, but the "crown of life" is for those who stand fast to the end (James 1 : 12).

3 : 12. "Put on, therefore, as the elect of God, . . . bowels of mercies." He that has put off the bowels of compassion, has put off the badge of election.

I THESSALONIANS.

In the first and second epistle to the Thessalonians there are twenty distinct references to the second coming of Christ.

At His first coming, Christ was a babe, a servant foretold by John the Baptist. Fishermen were His apostles. He was a mediator, a man, Christ; yet He was spit upon and crucified.

At his second coming, King of kings, heralded by the trump of archangels. Angels and archangels will be His servants and attendants, Judge, Lord of all.

1: 3. Three things:—
Work of faith.
Labor of love.
Patience of hope.

6. Followers.
7. Ensamples.
8. Echoes.

10. A coming Saviour, or a coming wrath. Which? If we love the seed of Abraham, if we love the burdened brute creation, if we love the heathen Gentile nations who know nothing of a Saviour, we shall joyfully welcome the hope of Christ's coming. For it is the hope that shall bring to the Jew his Messiah; to the creature his emancipation from man's dominion; to mute nature her freedom from thorns and thistles; to the heathen idolater a knowledge of God; to the waiting Bride the personal presence of the Bridegroom; to Jesus his kingdom and throne.

5 : 23. "Your body is the temple of the Holy Ghost." 1 Cor. 6 19.

> The "outer court" is the body.
> The "holy place" is the soul.
> The "holy of holies" is the spirit.

In unregenerate man the holy of holies is dark and untenanted. Man becomes sanctified when the Holy Spirit fills his spirit, and working through the soul, holds the body in obedience.

II THESSALONIANS.

3 : 10. An old Jewish proverb says: "He who brings up a child to no trade, brings up a child for the devil."

I TIMOTHY.

Luther's advice to a young preacher:—
> Stand up cheerfully.
> Speak out manfully.
> Leave off speedily.

Secker's plan of constructing a sermon:—
> First, explanation of that which is doctrinal.
> Second, application of that which is practical.

The former is like cutting a garment out; the latter is like putting the garment on.

6 : 5. R. V., "Supposing that godliness is a way of gain."

6. He is not a poor man that hath but little, but he is a poor man that wants much.

9. Not riches, but the desire to be rich, ⎫
10. Not money, but the love of money, ⎬ censured.
17. Not riches, but trust in riches, ⎭

6 : 10. *Money speculations* cause some } to err from
20, 21. *Scientific speculations* cause others } the faith

15. King of kings — that is King of Christians; because he "hath made us kings and priests unto God and his Father."

II TIMOTHY.

Hold fast the form of sound words.   Chap. 1 : 13.
Strive not about words.   2 : 14.
Rightly dividing the word of truth.   2 : 15.

2 :   Titles applied to Christians, in chapter 2: —
   1. Son.   V. 1.
   2. Faithful men, etc.   V. 2.
   3. Soldier.   V. 3.
   4. Wrestler.   V. 5.
   5. Husbandman, partaker of the fruits.   V. 6.
   6. Elect.   V. 10.
   7. Workman.   V. 15
   8. Vessel.   V. 21.
   9. Servant of the Lord.   V. 24.

All of these are alive, except the "vessel."

1. This chapter begins with sonship (v. 1), and ends with service (vs 24–26).   There must be life before there can be work.

15. "Rightly dividing the word of truth." The term is sacrificial, and refers to the orderly manner in which the sacrifices were to be cut up. See Lev. 1.

2 : 19. If iniquity be evil, why is it so much practised? If good, why so little professed?

21. The Master will only employ clean vessels to convey the water of life to thirsty souls.

3 : 15. Scripture knowledge is the candle without which faith cannot see to do its work.

4 : 2. "Preach the Word"—What word?—When?—How?—Why?

6. Present—"The time of my departure is at hand."

7. Past—"I have fought a good fight."

8. Future—"Henceforth there is laid up for me a crown of righteousness."

7. A child cried because the eggs were all broken when the chickens were hatched. But they had accomplished their work.

10. God's fence is too low to keep a graceless heart in bounds when the game is before him. Jude 11.

TITUS.

Threefold manifestation:—
    His word. Chap. 1 : 3.
    His grace. 2 : 11.
    His glory. 2 13.

Sound doctrine. Chap. 1 : 9, 2 : 1.
Sound in faith. 1 · 13, 2 . 2.
Sound speech. 2 : 8.

Chap. 1 : 16. "Unto every good work reprobate."
2 : 7. "A pattern of good works."

> Chap. 2 : 14. "Zealous of good works."
> 3 : 1, 5. "Ready to every good work."
> 3 : 8. "Careful to maintain good works."
> 3 : 14. "Learn to maintain good works."

2 : 11. Grace hath appeared. }
   13. Glory shall appear. }

> In fifty-three places where hope is referred to in the Bible, it relates to Christ's second coming.

3 : 2. A child once said to his mother, "You never speak ill of any one. I think you would have something good to say of the devil." "Well," she said, "imitate his perseverance."

HEBREWS.

In Hebrews —
> Sin is met by Atonement. Chap. 1 : 3.
> Guilt is met by justification. 2 : 9.
> Defilement is met by sanctification 2 : 11.
> Alienation is met by reconciliation. 2 : 17.
> Temptation is met by succor. 2 : 18.

Christ communicates eternity of existence to everything he touches: —
> His throne is forever and ever. Heb. 1 : 8.
> His salvation is eternal. 5 : 9.
> His priesthood is unchangeable. 7 : 24.
> His redemption is eternal. 9 : 12.
> His inheritance is eternal. 9 : 15.
> His kingdom cannot be moved. 12 : 28.
> His covenant is everlasting. 13 : 20.
> He is Himself the same, yesterday, to-day, and forever. 13 : 8.

"*Better things*" in Hebrews:—
>Better hope. Chap. 7 : 19.
>Better Testament. 7 : 22.
>Better covenant. 8 · 6.
>Better promises. 8 · 6.
>Better sacrifices. 9 23.
>Better substance. 10 : 34.
>Better resurrection. 11 : 35.
>Better country. 11 16.
>Better things. 12 24.

2 : 1. Note the margin, "leaky vessels." How can you keep a leaky vessel full? Keep it under a flowing fountain.

   3. One of the unanswered questions— "How shall we escape, if we neglect so great salvation?

3 : 7. The to-morrow of eternity is decided by the to-day, when we hear His voice.

    If God's to-day be too soon for thy repentance, thy to-morrow may be too late for God's acceptance.

    Mercy's clock does not always strike at our beck.

4 : 3. The Rest of belief.

   4. The Rest of creation.

   9. The Rest that remaineth to the people of God.

  11. The Rest of the soul.

  16. When you send letters to a foreign country, you send them *via* such and such a steamer or city. When you send good wishes to a friend, send them *via* the throne of grace.

6 : 4. The apostate does not lose the grace he had, but discovers he never had any.

12. God makes a promise.
Faith believes it.
Hope anticipates it
Patience quietly awaits it.

19. Hope is a good anchor, but it needs something to grip. Anchor to the throne and then shorten the rope.

9 : 22. *Essential conditions* —
Without shedding of blood, no remission. Chap. 9:22.

Without faith, impossible to please God. Chap. 11: 6.

Without holiness, no seeing God. Chap. 12 14

24. *Three appearances of Jesus* —
Present — "Now to appear in the presence of God for us"
Past — "He hath appeared to put away sin
Future — "Unto them that look for him he shall appear the second time"

10 : 19. Under the law, it was death to go behind the veil; under grace, it is death not to do so.

22. Truth in heart. Heb. 10 22.
Truth in word   Zech. 8:16.
Truth in deed. 2 Kings 20: 3.

32. Inward light, then outward fight.

10·37. Dean Alford translates this verse "Yet a very little while, and the Coming One will come, and will not tarry."

11: 1. Faith — the golden link binding us to every promise of God. There are three things necessary to it: —

Knowledge.
Assent.
Consent, or laying hold.

Abel witnesses to the atoning blood. V. 4.
Enoch witnesses to fellowship with God. V. 5
Noah witnesses to redemption. V. 7.
Abram witnesses to separation. V. 8.

8. Abraham did not know *whither* he went, but he knew *with whom* he went.

13. Build your nest upon no tree here, for God hath sold the forest to death, and every tree whereon we would rest is ready to be cut down, to the end that we may fly and mount up and build upon the Rock.

Flying birds are never taken in a fowler's snare.

25. The cream of earth's pleasures floats on the top He who is not content to skim it, but thinks by deeper draughts to attain more, fares worse.

The world always presents a deadly potion in the gilded cup of worldly pleasure.

The pleasures of sin are but for a season, but the punishment of unpardoned sin is everlasting.

38. Believers are worthies of whom the world is not worthy.

12 : 1. Let us "lay aside every weight."
    Secular **W**ork
   Worldly **E**njoyments
    Self-**I**ndulgence
      Greed
    False **H**umility
     Trifling.

2. The highest point in Hebrews — "Looking unto Jesus."

It is but little joy that can enter us here, because of our narrow capacity: but in heaven we shall enter into joy as vessels put into a sea of happiness.

6. Affliction from God exposeth to impatience. }
Affliction for God exposeth to pride.

The more a stone is wounded by the hand of the engraver, the greater beauty is produced.

14. Holiness is that which the sinner scorns and the Saviour crowns.

17. "No place of repentance," i. e., to undo the past is irrevocable, but not irreparable.

JAMES.

James is the apostle of action.

1 : 2. Temptations that find us dwelling in God are to our faith like winds that more firmly root the tree.

5. We may receive light either —
   a. As here, by asking God for wisdom;
   b. By being secretly persuaded as Artaxerxes was by Nehemiah; or

  c. By outward circumstances, as when Saul was led to Samuel by means of straying asses.

1 : 15. A tame leopard drew blood from its master's hand while licking it. It's old nature revived and it had to be shot.

  Sin is like a river, which begins in a quiet spring and ends in a stormy sea.

17. "No variableness." God's character does not change. A father punishes his child, if disobedient, but does not stop loving. Society punishes crime, because it does not change, and crime is contrary to its character.

  God remains unchangeable in his character and attitude toward sin; but when man changes, their relative attitude is changed. God changes in his dealings with a changed man.

2 : 5. The poor man may be rich in faith. The rich should be rich in good works.

10. We divide up *sin* into *sins* and miss the gravity.

  God gave one law, consisting of ten commandments.

  The golden chain of obedience is broken if one link is missing. If you are hanging over a precipice by a chain and one link goes, you are lost.

17. Faith without works God never regards. }
Works without faith God never rewards. }

  Some one said to Spurgeon. "I hear you are opposed to works" "No," he said, "I am not, nor to chimney pots; but I would not put them at the foundation."

Faith justifies us in the sight of God. }
Works justify us in the sight of men. }

Faith without works is like a man putting all his money into the foundation of his house. Works without faith is like a man building without any foundation.

A working faith is more than faith in works.

2:26. Idle grace soon becomes active corruption.

3:2. His heart cannot be pure whose tongue is not clean.

4:6. Give me the homely vessel of humility which God shall preserve and fill with the wine of his grace, rather than the varnished cup of pride which he will dash in pieces like a potter's vessel.

10. Self-humiliation must be real (Ps. 78:36, 37), and should be secret. Matt. 6:17, 18.

"Humble we must be, if to heaven we go:
High is the roof there, but the gate is low."

17. The sins of ignorance are most numerous: but the sins of knowledge are most dangerous.

5:16. Fervency in prayer by the power of the Holy Spirit is a good preservative against thoughts rushing in. Flies never settle on a boiling pot.

I PETER.

Peter's "precious" things:—
1 Pet. 1:7. Trial of faith much more precious.

1 Pet. 1:19. The precious blood of Christ.
    2:4, 6. The living stone, precious.
    2:7. He (Christ) is precious.
2 Pet. 1:1. Precious faith.
    1:4. Precious promises.
Peter speaks of "suffering," seventeen times in this epistle.

1:19. The precious blood of Christ.
Why *precious* ?
1. Because it redeems us. 1 Pet. 1:19.
2. Because it brings us nigh. Eph. 2:13.
3. Because it blots out our sins. Rev. 1:5.
4. Because it brings peace. Col. 1:20.
5. Because it justifies. Rom. 5 9.
6. Because it cleanses from all sin. 1 John 1:7.
7. Because it gives boldness in the day of judgment.

Christ left nothing behind on earth but his blood

2: 5. Accepted service.
20. Accepted suffering.

21. Plato said, "When men speak evil of you, live so that no man will believe it." But he did not tell how to do so.

24. The Christian's death is when he dies to sin.
No second death.

3:15. A Christian worker once said to a man, "God does not want your learning." "No," said the other, "nor your ignorance either."

4 : 14. If the world has nothing to say against you, Christ will have little to say for you.

II PETER.

1 : 4. In regeneration, the corruption is escaped. }
In reformation, only the pollution is escaped. }

6. Temperance is the virtue of prosperity.

Temperance — moderation — is the silken string running through the pearl chain of all the virtues.

19. The Bible does not say, as many seem to think, that prophecy is a dark place which we will do well to avoid, but rather that it is like a light shining in a dark place.

3 : 18. Many Christians say, "If I can take a back-seat in heaven, I shall be satisfied." But is God satisfied?

"Grow in grace" The old age of grace is maturity, not decay; advance, not decline; perfection, not imbecility. We go from strength to strength.
Without grace, there can be no saving knowledge.

I JOHN.

1 : 1. Voice — presence — touch of Christ.

7. Forgetfulness is not the cure for sin. Time cannot heal our iniquity. Gen. 42: 21.

You can find no means of touching your whole past life; but *God* can. "The blood of Jesus Christ his Son cleanseth us from *all* sin."

1 : 9. Full confession brings conviction from an earthly judge, but secures pardon from God. We are forgiven on account of God's *justice*, not merely mercy, because Jesus paid the price.

Unconfessed sin in the soul is like a bullet in the body.

It is better to be saved by divine mercy than sued by divine justice.

2 : 1. A saint is not free *from* sin — that is his burden; but he is not free *to* sin — that is his blessing. Sin is in him, but his soul is not in sin. A field of wheat may be good, and yet have weeds in it.

15. A true Christian loves not the world, yet he loves all the world.

"The things that are in the world," are like shadows in a pool. The higher the object, the lower the shadow. So things that are highest in this world's estimation are lowest in heaven (gold is valued highly here, but they pave the streets with it in heaven, Rev. 21·21); and the things that are lowest in this world's estimation are highest there (service is ignoble here, but in heaven they spend their time in service. Rev. 22: 3).

Study to fill your mind, rather than your coffers, knowing that gold and silver were originally mingled with dirt, until avarice or ambition parted them.

16. Millions have died of the wound of the eye.

2 : 17. The world is like a floating island, and as sure as we anchor to it, we shall be carried away by it.

"Know," in chapter 3 . —

V. 2. "We *know* that when He shall appear, we shall be like Him."

V. 5. "Ye *know* that He was manifested to take away our sins."

V. 14. We *know* that we have passed from death unto life"

V. 15. "Ye *know* that no murderer hath eternal life abiding in him."

V. 19. "We *know* that we are of the truth."

V. 24. "We *know* that He abideth in us."

3 : 3. Hope is too pure a plant to grow or flourish in an impure soul.

4. "Sin is the transgression of the law." Crossing the death-line : that is transgression.

5 : 5. Unbroken fellowship means uninterrupted success.

14. Promise — prayer — performance — are three links in the chain of blessing. If the middle link is missing, we have no right to expect the third.

15. It is a serious thing to pray ! We may be taken at our word.

JUDE.

24. "Perhaps he won't hold out." Is that your rule of life? then you cannot rejoice at the birth of a babe, lest it die: nor at its first smile, for it may one day frown.

REVELATION.

2 : 3. Not he that takes the field, but he that keeps it, not he that sets out, but he that holds out, deserves the name of saint.

3 : 17. Man's opinion of himself, and God's opinion of him: "Thou sayest, I am rich and increased with goods, and have need of nothing: and knowest not that thou art wretched, and miserable, and poor, and blind, and naked."

A D 64. Paul's conflict for Laodicea. Col. 2:1.

A. D. 64 Epaphras's zeal for Laodicea. Col. 4:13.

A. D. 96. Wretched and miserable Laodiceans. Rev 3 17.

20. "Behold I stand at the door and knock." The latch of the door is on the inside.

Who are my guests?

5 : 6. The only knowledge of sins in heaven will be by the evidences of God's provision for its pardon, and the sweet recollection of its forgiveness, by the redeemed.

7 : 14. Washed white, not whitewashed.

15. There is no weariness in heavenly service, but no rest in hell. Chap. 14: 11.

14 : 1. The beast permitted some to have the mark blazoned on the palms of their hands instead of the forehead (chap. 13:16), but no one must be ashamed of God's mark.

The man who bears a mark on his brow is the only man who does not see it.

16 : 13. The devil's trinity.

20 : 10. The devil entered at the beginning of the Bible, and is now cast out.

21 : We know four facts about the final re-genesis of the world, succeeding the millennium:—
   1. The earth shall be baptized with fire. 2 Pet. 3:7.
   2. No more sea. Rev. 21 1
   3. The New Jerusalem shall descend to earth. Rev. 21·2, 10
   4. Every vestige of sin shall be eliminated, and all conditions will be new.

13. The New Jerusalem, "on the east three gates; on the north three gates; on the south three gates; and on the west three gates." "In every denomination and church there are men who make one gate for *themselves* and then demand that all the world shall go through it."

16. The New Jerusalem is square, and it takes square men to fill it.

21. There is no place in heaven for the miser: he would want to pull up the golden pavement!

22 : 1. The River of God is full of water; but there is not one drop of it that takes its rise in earthly springs.

THE WATER OF LIFE.

Its character:—
Living water. John 4:10.
Clear. Rev. 22:1.

Pure   Rev. 22 1.
Abundant.   Eze. 47. 1–9.
Free   Rev. 21:6.
For whom provided:—
The thirsty   Rev 21:6.
Whosoever will   Rev. 22:17.
How to obtain it·—
Come.   Rev. 22:17.
Take.   Rev. 22:17.

22:17.   "Come thou." The Bible closes with a personal, individual appeal.
God says, "Come."   Gen. 7:1.
Jesus says, "Come."   Matt. 11:28.
The Spirit, the Church, he that heareth—say, "Come."   Rev. 21:17.
The sinner says, Come, Lord   Ps. 70:5
The first "Come" brought salvation to Noah and his family.

MISCELLANEOUS.

If we are quiet, we shall hear.   Eccl. 9 : 7.
If we hear, we shall be quiet.   Prov. 1 : 33.

TWO MISTAKES ABOUT JESUS.

His parents thought He was present when he was absent. Luke 2 : 44.

Mary thought He was absent when He was present. John 20 : 15.

A *friend* of publicans and sinners.   Luke 7 . 34.

This man *receiveth* sinners and eateth with them.   Luke 15 : 2.

Gone to be a *guest* with a man that is a sinner.   Luke 19 : 7; Rev. 3 : 20.

MOUNTAIN SCENES IN SCRIPTURE.

Gen. 22:2. As sinners we see substitution.

Ex. 17:10. As warriors we obtain victory.

Ex. 24:1–9. As worshipers in the presence of God.

1 Kings 18:42. As intercessors on behalf of others.

Mark 9:2. As privileged friends we see God's glory.

Rev. 21:10. As waiting ones we look by faith on things that are eternal.

THE WILL OF GOD IN LIFE.

Do you seek for an object in life?
   Heb: 10: 7. "I come to do thy will, O God."

Do you seek for food in life?
> John 4:34. "My meat is to do the will of Him that sent me."

Do you seek for society?
> Mark 3:35. "Whosoever shall do the will of God, the same is my brother, and sister, and mother." (R. V.)

Do you seek for education?
> Ps. 143:10. Teach me to do thy will, for thou art my God."

Do you seek for pleasure?
> Ps. 40:8. "I delight to do thy will, O my God."

Do you seek for a reward?
> 1 John 2:17. "He that doeth the will of God abideth forever."

Do you seek to know the will of God?
> 1 Thess. 4:3. "This is the will of God, even your sanctification."
>
> 1 Thess. 5:16–18. "Rejoice alway; pray without ceasing, in everything give thanks: for this is the will of God in Christ Jesus to you-ward." (R. V.)

Do you seek assurance?
> John 7:17. "If any man willeth to do His will, he shall know of the teaching." (R. V.)

Do you seek for power in prayer?
> 1 John 5:14. "If we ask anything according to His will, He heareth us." (R. V.)

Christianity in doctrine is — union with Christ.
    "   " experience is — realization thereof.
    "   " practice is — manifestation thereof.

If doctrine only, it leads to antinomianism.
If experience only, it leads to enthusiasm.
If practice only, it leads to Pharisaism.

God revealed — in nature. Gen. 1:1.
  in man. Gen. 1:26.
  in Christ. Col. 2:9.

  in nature as Creator.
  in history as Providence.
  in humanity as Father.

God loves us: as a mother. Isa. 66:13.
  as a father. Ps. 103:13.
  as a brother. Prov. 17:17.
  as a friend. Prov. 18:24.

CHRIST THE PROPHET.

Acts 3:22. God raised Him up.
Luke 4:18. He was annointed.
John 17:8. He spake the words of God.
John 1:18. He revealed God.
Luke 24·19. He was called a prophet.
Mark 13:23. He foretold the future.
Rev. 3:14. He was a faithful witness.

CHRIST THE KING.

Ps. 2:6. God called him King.
John 19·19. Pilate called him King.
Rev. 3:21. He is now on a throne.
Rev. 19:16. He appears as King.
Rev 15:3. He is King of nations.
Zech. 14:9. He is King over all the earth.
Heb 1:8 His scepter is a right scepter.

WHAT THE WORD OF GOD DOES.

1 Pet. 1:23. By it we are born again.
1 Pet. 2:2. By it we grow.
John 15:3. By it we are cleansed.
John 17:17. By it we are sanctified.
Ps. 119:105. By it we get light.
Eph. 6:17. By it we are defended.
John 12:48. By it man is judged.

SPIRITUAL CALCULATION.

Acts 20:24. "I count not my life dear unto me."
Phil. 3:7. "I count all things but loss and dung."
Phil. 3:13. "I count not to have apprehended."
Rom. 8:18. "I reckon that the sufferings of this present time are not worthy to be compared to the glory that shall be revealed"
Rom. 6:11. "Reckon yourselves dead unto sin."
James 1:2. "Count it all joy when ye fall into divers temptations"
James 5:11. "We count them happy which endure."
Acts 5:41. The disciples counted it joy that they were "worthy to suffer shame for His name."

God met — Adam in the garden,
    Enoch in his daily walk,
    Abram under the oak,
    Jacob at the brook,
    Moses at the bush,
    Joshua at Jericho.

Five crowns for believers : —
  1. A crown of life, for endurance. James 1:12; Rev. 2:10.
  2. A crown of righteousness, for the good fight of faith. 2 Tim. 4:8.
  3. A crown of rejoicing, for winning souls. 1 Thess. 2:19.
  4. A crown of glory, for those who edify the church, and for feeding souls. 1 Pet. 5:4.
  5. A crown of reward, for those who successfully run the race. 1 Cor. 9:25.

DISTINGUISHING TRAITS.

Obedient Romans.	Rejoicing Philippians.
Carnal Corinthians.	Faithful Colossians.
Legal Galatians.	Loving Thessalonians.
Heavenly-minded Ephesians.	Dwarfed Hebrews.

The Lord God may be known, —
  1. By the noise of his footsteps. 2 Sam. 15:24.
  2. By the thunder which accompanies His approach. Ex. 9.23, Job 37:4, 5; Ps. 29:3, 9.
  3. By the sound of his voice. Gen. 3:8.

What God does with the sins of his people.
  Remembers them no more. Jer. 31:34.
  Covers them. Ps. 32.1.
  Removes them as far as the east is from the west. Ps. 103:12.

Casts them behind his back. Isa 38: 17.
Blots them out   Isa. 44 22.
Casts them into the depths of the sea.   Micah 7: 19.
Pardons them. Jer 33 8.
Seeks for and cannot find them. Jer 50: 20.

A lamb.   Ex. 3 : 3 .... A Saviour.   Luke 2 : 11.
The lamb.   " 3 . 4 .... The Saviour.   John 4 : 42.
Your Lamb. " 3 : 5 .... My Saviour.   Luke 1 : 47.

CHILDREN'S QUESTIONS.
Psalm 78 : 3-8.

Respecting the Passover. Ex. 12 : 26. Redemption and Deliverance.

Respecting the feast of unleavened bread. Ex. 13 . 8. Separation from evil.

Respecting the redemption of the firstborn. Ex. 13 : 14. Consecration.

Respecting the law and testimonies Deut. 6 : 20, 21. Obedience.

Respecting the stones taken out of Jordan. Joshua 4 : 6, 7. Resurrection life.

CANDLES OF SCRIPTURE.

1. *The candle of the law:* Conscience. Prov. 20 : 27 ; Ps. 18 : 28.
2. *The candle of grace:* Love. Luke 15 : 8.
3. *The candle of Testimony:* Life. Matt. 5 : 15. Shining for God's glory (verse 16) in the world. Phil. 2 : 15
4. *The candle extinguished:* Death. Job 18 : 6 ; 21 : 17.
5. *The candle outshone:* Glory. Rev. 22 : 5.

HIS SHED BLOOD.

Justified	by His blood	....	Rom. 5 : 9.
Sanctified	" " "	....	Heb. 13 :12.
Redeemed	" " "	....	Eph. 1 : 7.
Forgiven	" " "	....	Matt. 26 : 28.
Purchased	" " "	....	Acts 20 : 28.
Brought near	" " "	....	Eph. 2 :13.
Peace	" " "	....	Col. 1 : 20.
Cleansed	" " "	....	1 John 1 : 7.
Victory	" " "	....	Rev. 12 : 11.
Purged	" " "	....	Heb. 9 : 14.

LAWS SET ASIDE.

Natural law was set aside for Joshua when the sun and moon stood still.   Josh. 10 : 12.

Physical law was set aside for Hezekiah when his life was prolonged fifteen years in answer to prayer.   Isa. 38 : 1–6.

Human law was set aside for Peter when he was released from the dungeon.   Acts 12 : 6–9.

YESTERDAY — TO-DAY — TO-MORROW.

"*Jesus Christ the same yesterday, and to-day, and forever.*" *Heb. 13 : 8.*

"For we are but of yesterday, and know nothing, because our days upon earth are a shadow."   Job. 8 : 9.

"To-day if ye will hear his voice, harden not your hearts."   Heb. 4 : 7.

"But exhort one another daily, while it is called to-day; lest any of you be hardened through the deceitfulness of sin."   Heb. 3 : 13.

"Boast not thyself of to-morrow; for thou knowest not what a day may bring forth." Prov. 27 · 1.

"Ye know not what shall be on the morrow. For what is your life? It is even a vapor, that appeareth for a little time, and then vanisheth away." James 4 : 14.

God's first recorded utterance to man · "Thou shalt *surely* die." Gen. 2 : 17.

His last recorded utterance to man: "*Surely* I come quickly." Rev. 22 : 20.

Man's first recorded utterance to God: "I was afraid . . . I hid myself." Gen. 3 : 10.

Man's last recorded utterance to God: "Even so, come, Lord Jesus." Rev. 22 : 20.

One's knowledge of God may be,—
1. Speculative or theoretical; embracing one's views respecting His existence, perfections, and will, but without power over the heart. James 4 : 17.
2. Saving; controlling the heart and conduct. John 17 : 3.

He who denies God, subverts all religion.
He who denies Christ, subverts the gospel.

JESUS CHRIST AS MEDIATOR.

A mediator is one who comes in between two parties who are at variance, in order to reconcile them.

1. Both parties must agree to accept him. God chose Christ from the foundation of the world. 1 Peter 1 : 20, 21. Do you accept him?

2. He should be the equal of both parties. Christ is both God and man.

3. He should understand the case. Christ knows God's will and rights ; and also man's sins and wants.

4. Both parties must agree to leave the case absolutely in his hands. God has committed all power into the hands of Christ. Do you ?

5. He should be desirous to bring the case to a happy settlement. Christ died to reconcile man to God.

"There is one God, and one mediator between God and men, the man Christ Jesus " 1 Tim. 2 : 5.

WHATSOEVER YE DO.

Do all to the glory of God. 1 Cor. 10 : 31.
" " in the name of the Lord Jesus. Col. 3 : 17.
" " heartily, as to the Lord. Col. 3 : 23.

All natural growth ends in decay ; but growth in the knowledge and love of God ends in glory and immortality

---

No one can write "A Life of Christ," because it is not yet finished.

Every sin is a fountain.

EPITAPH IN A GRAVEYARD IN ENGLAND.

I have sinned ;
I have repented ;
I have trusted ;
I have loved ;
I rest ;
I shall rise ;
I shall reign.

Grace does not run in the blood, like corruption.

Men will wrangle for religion, write for it, fight for it, die for it, anything but live for it.

We ought to confess Christ,—
>For the world's sake,
>For the church's sake,
>For our own sake,
>For Christ's sake.

Bearing rule over body.   1 Cor. 9 : 27.
"   "   "   soul.   2 Cor. 10 : 5.
"   "   "   spirit.   Prov. 16 : 32.

THINGS THAT TEND TO POVERTY.

Withholding more than is meet............	Prov. 11 : 24.
Refusing instruction.....................	" 13 : 18.
Idle talking............................	" 14 : 23.
Love of sleep..........................	" 20 : 13.
Oppressing the poor and giving to the rich..	" 22 : 16.
Drunkenness, gluttony, and drowsiness......	" 23 : 21.
Following after vain persons.............	" 28 : 19.
Hastening to be rich....................	" 28 : 22.
Living far from Joseph's storehouses.......	Gen. 45 : 11.

"AGONIZE."
Used eight times in New Testament.

In prayer.   Col. 4 : 12.   Translated "labor fervently."
As a workman.   Col. 1 : 29.   Translated "strive."

As a wrestler to gain the prize. 1 Cor. 9 : 25. Translated "strive."

As a soldier. 1 Tim. 6 : 12 ; 4 : 7. Translated "fight."

As a man who defends his friend from danger. John 18 : 36. Translated "fight."

For salvation. Luke 13 : 24. Translated "strive."

As the Lord Himself in Gethsemane. Luke 22 : 44. Translated "agony."

Our faith must be tested. God builds no ships but what He sends to sea.

Sin killed Jesus Christ. Let Him kill sin.

As sleeps the oak within the acorn, so sleeps heaven within the first cry, "Abba, Father"

UNLESS.

I had *fainted* unless I had believed. Ps. 27 : 13.

Unless the Lord had been my help, my soul had almost dwelt *in silence*. Ps. 94 : 17.

Unless thy law had been my delights, I should then have *perished* in mine affliction. Ps. 119 : 92.

CLEAN HANDS.

For strength. Job 17 : 9.

For reward. 2 Sam. 22 : 21 ; Ps. 18 : 20, 24.

For acceptance. Ps. 24 : 3, 4.

For worship. Ps. 26 : 6.

For humbling. James 4 : 8.

THE TEMPLE BUILT

At Jerusalem (the place or possession of peace). 2 Chron. 3 : 1.

In Mount Moriah (the manifestation or sight of Jehovah). Gen. 22 : 2.

Where the father spared not his son. Gen. 22 : 12; Rom. 8 : 32.

Where God said, It is enough. 1 Chron. 21 : 15 ; John 19 : 30

Where the angel sheathed his sword. 1 Chron. 21 : 27 ; Zech. 13 : 7.

Where corn was threshed. 2 Chron. 3 : 1 ; Isa. 53 : 10.

The wicked are like,—
    Bird's caught in a snare. Eccl. 9 : 12.
    Fishes taken in the net. Eccl. 9 : 12.
    Sheep laid in the grave. Ps. 49 : 14.
    Deaf adder. Ps. 58 : 4.
    Ravening lion. Ps. 17 : 12.

They that trust in the Lord are like,—
    A tree planted by the waters. Jer. 17 : 8.
    A green olive tree. Ps. 52 : 8.
    A green fir tree. Hosea 14 : 8.
    The palm tree. Ps. 92 : 12.
    A cedar in Lebanon. Ps. 92 : 12.
    A vine. Hosea 14 : 7.
    Willows. Isa. 44 : 4.
    A shock of corn. Job 5 : 26.
    The lily among thorns. Song of Solomon 2 : 2.
    A branch. Prov. 11 : 28.

The wicked are like,—
    Heath in the desert. Jer. 17 : 6.
    A brier. Micah 7 : 4.
    A green bay tree. Ps. 37 : 35.
    Grass, green herb. Ps. 37 : 2.
    The chaff. Ps. 1 : 4.
    The stubble. Ps. 83 : 13.

SPIRITUAL BANKRUPTCY.

When the woman had *spent all*, she came to Jesus. Mark 5 : 26.

When the prodigal had *spent all*, he came to his father. Luke 15 : 14.

When the Egyptians had *spent all*, they came to Joseph. Gen. 47 : 18.

When the two debtors had *nothing to pay*, the creditor forgave them both. Luke 7 : 42

The doctrines of grace, although they may be very healing, are at first very humbling.

CHRIST IN THE GOSPELS.

Matthew : The son of David. "Behold thy King." Zech. 9 : 9.

Mark : The servant of Jehovah. "Behold my servant." Isa. 42 : 1.

Luke : The Son of man. "Behold the man." Zech. 6 : 12.

John : The Son of God. "Behold your God." Isa. 40 : 9.

CHRIST THE BRANCH.

Matthew: "I will raise *unto David* a righteous *Branch*, and *a King* shall reign." Jer. 23:5.
Mark: "My *Servant* the *Branch*." Zech. 3:8.
Luke: "Behold the *man* whose name is the *Branch*." Zech. 6:12.
John: "In that day shall the *branch of the Lord* be beautiful and glorious." Isa. 4:2.

The Son in the bosom of the Father. John 1:18.
The sinner in the " " " Son. " 13:25.

We beheld His glory. John 1:14. Past.
Beholding His glory. 2 Cor. 3:18. Present.
That they may behold my glory. John 17:24. Future.

Prayer: "Be not silent to me." Ps. 28:1.
Promise: "Our God shall come and shall not keep silence." Ps. 50:3.

Some church-members have their roots on the church side of the fence, but their boughs stretch over the wall and drop the fruit into the world.

If you lean out of the perpendicular, lean toward Christ.

The cloak of a false profession will make an awful blaze when God burns up the stubble.

"HE WILL KEEP THE FEET OF HIS SAINTS." 1 Sam. 2:9.

Keep them shod. Eph. 6 : 15.
Keep them from falling. Jude 24 ; Ps. 116 : 8.
Keep them clean. John 13 : 5, 6.
Guide them in the way of peace. Luke 1 : 79.
Pluck them out of the net. Ps. 25 : 15.
Set them on a rock. Ps. 40 : 2.
Light them upon their path. Ps. 119 : 105.
Bring them within His gates. Ps. 122 : 2.

"THIS GOD IS OUR GOD."

The God of Peace. Phil. 4 : 9.
The God of Love. 2 Cor. 13 : 11.
The God of Pardon. Neh. 9 : 17.
The God of Salvation. Isa. 12 : 2.
The God of Patience and Consolation. Rom. 15 : 5.
The God of Hope. Rom. 15 : 13.
The God of all Comfort. 2 Cor. 1 : 3.
The God of all Grace. 1 Peter 5 : 10.
The God of Glory. Acts 7 : 2.

No inheritance without sonship,
No sonship without spiritual birth,
No spiritual birth without Christ,
No Christ without faith.

Atheism gives liberty, but destroys order.
Superstition gives order, but destroys liberty.
Christ gives both order and liberty.

CONTRAST GOD'S THOUGHTS OF MAN WITH MAN'S THOUGHTS OF GOD:—

God yearned over the poor wanderer; man looked on God as a hard master.

God sent His only begotten Son to ransom man; man offered thirty pieces of silver for Him.

God's thoughts are toward man in reconciliation; man's are away from God, heedless of His favors.

When Jesus comes the second time, there will be no mistake as to His identity.

Man's order: "Seeing is Believing."
God's order: "Believing is Seeing." John 11 : 40.
"Jesus said unto her, Said I not unto thee that if thou wouldest believe, thou shouldest see the glory of God?"

"Crowns are being distributed to-day, and I am going to receive one," said a dying martyr as she was being put to death.

IF NOT, WHY NOT?

You call me *master*, and you do not question me.
You call me *the light*, and you do not look to me.
You call me *the way*, and you do not follow me.
You call me *the truth*, and you do not believe me.
You call me *the life*, and you do not wish for me.
You call me *the wise*, and you give me no attention.
You call me *lovely*, and you do not love me.
You call me *rich*, and you do not ask for anything.

You call me *the everlasting*, and you do not seek me.
You call me *merciful*, and you do not trust me.
You call me *almighty*, and you do not honor me.
You call me *righteous*, and you do not fear me.

What have I done ?   Jer. 8 : 6.
How wilt thou do ?   Jer. 12 : 5.
What wilt thou say ?   Jer. 13 : 21.

WHAT CANNOT BE FULLY KNOWN.

The love of Christ, which passeth knowledge.   Eph. 3 : 19.
The peace of God which passeth understanding.   Phil 4 : 7.
The ways of God, which are past finding out.   Rom. 11: 33

THREE STORMS.

1. The storm of Jonah (chap. 2), which was sent as a punishment against Jonah for his sin, ceasing only when he was cast into the sea. Type of Jesus who could say, "All thy waves and thy billows are gone over me." Ps 42 : 7.
2. The storm in Acts (chap. 27), which did not cease, but a message from the Lord was sent to comfort His people in the midst of it. Picture of believers who in the midst of fierce tossings are encouraged by His word, knowing that they are "drawing near to some country" (Acts 27 : 27), "that is, an heavenly Heb. 11 : 16.
3. The storm in Mark (chap. 4), which was stilled at once by the word of Jesus. Picture of the great calm He commands within the believer's heart.

FOUR GREAT SIGHTS.

The sight that God had : "God looked down . . . to see . . ." Ps. 53 : 2.

The sight that man had : "And all the people that came together to that sight, beholding . . ." Luke 23 : 48.

The sight that believers have : "We see Jesus." Heb. 2 : 9.

The sight that all men shall have : "Behold, He cometh . . . every eye shall see him." Rev. 1 : 7.

THE CHRISTIAN'S SEVENFOLD POSITION.

God has conferred upon believers a sevenfold position which cannot be sinned away, but which is dependent upon their practical state for its enjoyment.

1. Relationship, for they are children. Rom. 8 : 16.
2. Fellowship, for they are brothers. John 20 : 17.
3. Dignity, for they are sons. Rom. 8 : 14.
4. Glory, for they are heirs. Rom. 8 · 17.
5. Separateness, for they are saints. 1 Cor. 1 : 2.
6. Nearness, for they are priests. 1 Peter 2 : 5.
7. Authority, for they are kings. Rev. 1 : 6.

Jesus on earth — His path, His spirit, His ways — is the measure of our walk and obedience.

THREE CLASSES.

The astonished — "When Jesus had ended these sayings, the people were astonished at his doctrine." Matt. 7 : 28.

The critical — "And he taught them in their synagogue, . . . and they said, Whence hath this man this wisdom ? . . . Is not this the carpenter's son ?" Matt. 13:54, 55.

The trembling — "As he reasoned of righteousness, temperance, and judgment to come, Felix trembled." Acts 24 : 25.

When Lot was safe out of Sodom, judgment came.
When Noah was safe in the ark, judgment came.
When the church is gathered home, judgment will come.

AS THE SAND.

Abraham's seed. Gen. 22 : 17.
Joseph's corn. Gen. 41 : 49.
David's seed. Jer. 33 : 22.
Solomon's largeness of heart. 1 Kings 4: 29.
God's thoughts unto us. Ps. 139: 18.

SATAN'S COUNTERFEITS.

The scarlet woman (Rev. 17) — the bride.
Babylon the great — The New Jerusalem.
A roaring lion — The lion of the tribe of Judah.
Barabbas (son of the father) — The Son of the Father.
Antichrist — Christ.
Lucifer, son of the morning — the bright and morning Star.

The compassion of Christ inclines Him to save sinners.
The power of Christ enables Him to save sinners.
The promises of Christ bind Him to save sinners.

Faith gives us living joy and dying rest.

Ever since sin entered the world, and death by sin, the earth has been a vast burying-ground for her children.

SPIRITUAL TRANSFORMATION.

"Predestinated to be conformed to the image of His Son." Rom. 8:29.

How the image is produced: —

    Moulding — in clay. Jer. 18:2, 6; Isa. 64:8; 45:9;
      "Lie still and let Him mould thee."— *Luther.*
    Sealing — in wax or clay. Job. 38:14; 2 Tim. 2:19
    Reflecting — in a mirror. 2 Cor. 3:18; Prov. 27:19.
    Engraving — in precious stones. Ex. 28:9–21.
    Writing on tablets. 2 Cor. 3:3.
    Stamping or casting — metals. Mark 12:16; 2 Chron. 4:17.
    Carving — in wood. 1 Kings 6:18; Ex. 31:5.

What preparation is needed: —

    The clay — dug up. Isa. 58:1.
    The wax — melted. Ps. 22:14; Ps. 97:5.
    The mirror — polished.
    "If the polish of the mirror were perfect, it would be invisible; we should simply see the image of what is reflected." — *Prof. Tyndall on "Reflection."*
    The stones — hewn, Isa. 51:1; 1 Kings 5:17; polished, Ps. 144:12.
    The precious stones — found, Job 28:6; prepared, 1 Chron. 29:2: cut and set. Ex. 31:5.

The metals — sought, Prov. 2:4; Job 28:1, 2, dug up, Job 28:2; melted, Prov. 17:3; purified, Mal. 3:3; Prov. 25:4.

The wood — hewn. 1 Kings 5:6; "Is not this the carpenter?" Mark 6:3.

THE LORD'S SILENCE.

Where is He silent ?

Before Caiaphas. ("Jesus held his peace." Matt. 26:63.) Heartless ecclesiasticism.

Before Herod. ("He answered him nothing." Luke 23:9.) Empty curiosity.

Before Pilate. ("Jesus gave him no answer." John 19:9.) Carping criticism.

To what is He silent ?

To hypocrisy. John 8·6. "This they said, tempting him."

To false accusation. Matt 15:2, 3, 5. "Why do thy disciples transgress the tradition of the elders?"

To foregone conclusions. John 19:9. "Whence art thou?"

What makes Him silent ?

Men's contempt. Prov. 1:22-28.

Men's carelessness. Song of Solomon 5:6.

Men's selfishness. Amos 8:4-12.

Men's sin. Isa. 1:15; Jer. 11:2.

When is He silent ?

In His love. Zeph. 3:17.

In His wisdom. Matt. 15:23.

In His power. Rev. 8:1.

Why is He silent?
 To arouse men's consciences. John 8.6, 8.
 To increase our earnestness. Matt. 15:23.
 To educate faith. Job. 23:8; Matt. 15:23.
 To teach humility. Matt 15:23.

To what is He not silent?
 The prayer of the penitent. Le 18:13; 2 Chron 7:14.
 The cry of the widow and orphan. Ex. 22:23.
 The voice of a child. Gen. 21:17.
 The desire for Himself. Prov. 8:17, Ps. 145:19.
 The cry of the needy. Ps. 12:5; 72.12.
 The praise of His people. 2 Chron. 5:13, 14.

The Spectrum of Love has nine ingredients (1 Cor. 13):—
 Patience — "Love suffereth long."
 Kindness — "And is kind."
 Generosity — "Love envieth not."
 Humility — "Love vaunteth not itself, is not puffed up."
 Courtesy — "Doth not behave itself unseemly."
 Unselfishness — "Seeketh not her own."
 Good Temper — "Is not easily provoked."
 Guilelessness — "Thinketh no evil."
 Sincerity — "Rejoiceth not in iniquity, but rejoiceth in the truth."

We have not to put out the eyes of our reason to see with the vision of faith; but if once we are sure that God has spoken, we are to do His will, whether we understand it or not.

IS THE LORD'S HAND SHORTENED?

Asked respecting the Father. Num. 11 : 23.
" " the Son. Isa. 50 : 2.
" " the Spirit. Micah 2 : 7.

WITH ALL YOUR HEART.

Seek the Lord. Deut. 4 : 29.
Serve the Lord. Deut. 10 : 12.
Love the Lord. Deut. 13 : 3.
Obey the Lord. Deut. 30 : 2.
Turn unto the Lord. Deut. 30 : 10.
Walk before the Lord. 1 Kings 2 : 4.
Follow the Lord. 1 Kings 14 : 8.
Praise the Lord. Ps. 86 : 12.
Trust the Lord. Prov. 3 : 5.

MIRRORS.

The laver made of mirrors. Ex. 38 : 8.
The Word a mirror —
    1. In which we see ourselves. James 1 : 23, 24.
    2. " " " " Him. 1 Cor. 13 : 12.
Believers are mirrors to reflect his image. 2 Cor. 3 : 18.

APPLY YOUR HEART.

To wisdom. Ps 90 : 12.
To understanding. Prov. 2 : 2.
To knowledge. Prov. 22 : 17.
To instruction. Prov. 23 : 12.

THE DISCIPLE WHOM JESUS LOVED.

Leaning on Jesus' bosom.   John 13 : 23.   The Rest of Love.

Witnessing His death.   John 19 : 26.   The Confidence of Love.

Running to the sepulchre.   John 20 : 2, 4.   The Activity of Love.

Recognizing the Lord.   John 21 : 7.   The Quicksightedness of Love.

Following Jesus.   John 21 : 20.   The Close Companionship of Love.

PRISONS THAT COULD NOT KEEP GOD OUT.

Joseph's.   Gen. 39 : 20, 21.   Mercy.
The Egyptian's.   Ex. 12 : 29.   Death.
Manasseh's.   2 Chron. 33 : 11–13.   Answer to prayer.
Jeremiah's.   Jer. 32 : 1 ; 33 : 1.   The word of prophecy.
Apostles'.   Acts 5 : 19.   Deliverance.
Peter's.   Acts 12 : 7.   Deliverance.
Paul's and Silas's.   Acts 16.
Paul's.   Eph. 3 : 1 ; 4 : 1 ; 2 Tim. 1 : 8 ; Philemon 1 : 9.

That which lies in the well of your thought will come up in the bucket of your speech.

THE LORD ON EVERY SIDE.

Delivering from enemies.   Judges 8 : 34.
Giving rest.   1 Kings 5 : 4 ; 2 Chron. 14 : 7.
Guiding.   2 Chron. 32 : 22.

Hedging about. Job 1 : 10.
Comforting. Ps. 71 : 21.
Gathering His people. Ezek. 37 : 21.

A GOOD LAND.

God's testimony : "A land that I had espied for them, flowing with milk and honey, which is the glory of all lands." Ezek. 20 : 6.

The spies' unwilling testimony : "We came unto the land whither thou sentest us, and surely it floweth with milk and honey." Num. 13 : 27.

The enemy's testimony : "A land of corn and wine, a land of bread and vineyards, a land of oil olive and of honey." 2 Kings 18 : 32.

GOD'S FINGER.

In creation. Ps. 8 : 3.
In the plagues. Ex. 8 : 19.
In casting out devils. Luke 11 : 20.

Writing on,—
    The tables of stone. Ex. 31 : 18.
    The wall of the palace. Dan. 5 : 5.
    The temple floor. John 8 : 6.
    Believers' hearts. 2 Cor. 3 : 2, 3.
    " minds. Heb. 10 : 16.
    " foreheads. Rev. 14 : 1.

God had one Son without sin, but He never had a son without trial.

THE PARABLE OF THE GOOD SAMARITAN.
(Luke 10:30)

A certain man— the whole human race.

Went down — fell.

From Jerusalem — the place of blessing. "In Salem also is His tabernacle, and His dwelling place in Zion." Ps. 76 2.

To Jericho — the place of the curse. "And Joshua adjured them at that time, saying, Cursed be the man before the Lord, that riseth up and buildeth this city Jericho." Josh. 6 26.

And fell among thieves — Satan and his angels.

Which stripped him of his raiment— Satan stripped man of his innocency.

And wounded him— a wound which brought death to mankind.

And departed— having set man going, Satan could leave him on his path. "A child left to himself bringeth his mother to shame." Prov. 29:15.

Leaving him half dead — dead in soul, mortal in body.

And by chance — that is, by coincidence.

A certain priest — the law.

Came down that way — going the same downward path. "None of them can by any means redeem his brother." Ps. 49·7.

And when he saw him, he passed by on the other side— unable or unwilling to help.

And likewise a Levite— ceremonials.

But a certain Samaritan— Jesus incarnate.

As he journeyed— it does not say "*down.*" Perhaps he was journeying up to Jerusalem.

Came where he was — became "partaker of flesh and blood." Heb. 2:14.

And when he saw him, he had compassion on him — just as Jesus had when He saw the bereaved widow of Nain. Luke 7:13.

And went to him, and bound up his wounds — "with his stripes we are healed," — at Calvary.

Pouring in oil and wine — at Pentecost.

And set him on his own beast — putting man in His own place. "And hath raised us up together, and made us sit together in heavenly places in Christ Jesus." Eph. 2:6.

And brought him to an inn — where all bonafide travelers were received.

And took care of him — knowing the negligence of the servants.

And on the morrow when he departed — to return to heaven.

He took out two pence — two gifts.

And gave them to the host — "But unto every one of us is given *grace* according to the measure of the *gift* of Christ." Eph. 4:7.

And said unto him, Take care of him — "Bear ye one another's burdens, and so fulfil the law of Christ." Gal. 6:2.

And whatsoever thou spendest over, I will repay thee — no care shown to wounded travelers is forgotten. "And the King shall answer and say unto them, Verily I say unto you, Inasmuch as ye have done it unto one of the least of these my brethren, ye have done it unto me." Matt. 25:40.

When I come again — His second coming.

PROMISES.

Every promise is built on four pillars : —
1. God's justice and holiness, which will not suffer Him to deceive.
2. His grace and goodness, which will not suffer Him to forget.
3. His truth, which will not suffer Him to change.
4. His power, which makes Him able to accomplish.

God's promises always sustain a trusting soul ; never a doubting one.

I am permitted to take salvation gratis — "Whosoever will." Rev. 22:17.

I am invited — "Come unto me." Matt. 11:28.

I am entreated — "As though God did beseech you." 2 Cor. 5:20.

I am commanded — "This is His commandment." 1 John 3:23.

I am finally compelled — "Compel them to come in." Luke 14:23.

SYMBOLISM OF THE ROCK.

1. God's strength : "In God is my salvation and my glory: the rock of my strength and my refuge is in God." Ps. 62:7.
2. God's protection : "Be thou my strong rock, for an house of defence to save me." Ps. 31:2.

3. God's salvation: "He shall cry unto me, Thou art my Father, my God, and the rock of my salvation." Ps. 89:26.
4. Christ's care · "For they drank of that spiritual rock that followed them; and that rock was Christ." 1 Cor. 10:4.
5. The church's foundation: "Thou art Peter, and upon this rock I will build my church." Matt. 16:18.

CHRIST'S THREE "I COMES."

Lo, I come (from heaven to earth). Ps. 40:7.
I come to thee (from earth to heaven). John 17:11.
I come quickly (from heaven to earth). Rev. 22:20.

God is love. 1 John 4:16. Walk in love. Eph. 5:2.
God is light. 1 John 1:5. Walk in the light. 1 John 1:7.
God is true. 2 Cor. 1·18. Walk in the truth. 3 John 4.

UPON CHRIST'S SHOULDERS.

As High Priest — the names of the tribes. Ex. 28:12.
As King — the government. Isa 9:6.
As Shepherd — the lost sheep. Luke 15:5.

"WHAT SHALL I DO?"

Asked by the people, the publicans, the soldiers who were under conviction. Luke 3:10, 12, 14. Answer: Repent.
Asked by a certain lawyer, in order to test Christ. Luke 10:25. Answer. Obey.

Asked by a certain rich man, in a spirit of avarice. Luke 12:17.
Asked by the unjust steward, under examination. Luke 16:3.
Asked by a certain ruler, in a spirit of inquiry. Luke 18 18. Answer Distribute
Asked by Jesus, in compassion Luke 18 41.
Asked by the Lord of the vineyard, in long suffering. Luke 20:13

A cake made out of memories will do for a bite now and then, but makes poor daily bread. We want the present enjoyment of God.

WITH ONE ACCORD.

Unanimity in prayer. Acts 1:14; 4:24.
Unanimity as to place. Acts 2:1, 46; 5:12.
Unanimity in giving heed to the word. Acts 8:6.
Unanimity as to peace in the church. Acts 15:25.
Unanimity in glorifying God. Rom. 15:6.
The way of the world —
    Unanimity in hatred and enmity against the truth. Joshua 9:2; Acts 7:57; 18:12; 19:29.
    Unanimity in diplomacy. Acts 12:20.

THE WORLD IS OURS. 1 COR. 3:22.

A field for sowing. John 4·35; 2 Cor. 9:6.
An arena for contest and race. 1 Cor. 9:25, 26.
A school in which we graduate. Isa. 54:13.
A desert for pilgrim experience. Song of Solomon 8:5; Heb. 11·13.

ONE THING.

Not *one thing* hath failed.   Joshua 23 : 14.   God's promises.
One thing have I desired.   Ps. 27 : 4.   Communion.
One thing befalleth.   Eccl. 3 . 19.   Death.
One thing lacking.   Mark 10 : 21.   Conversion.
One thing needful.   Luke 10 42.   The listening ear.
One thing I know   John 9 : 25.   Assurance.
One thing I do.   Phil. 3 : 13.   Progress.
Be not ignorant of this *one thing*.   2 Peter 3 : 8.   The Lord's return.

Demas fell, through the world.   2 Tim. 4 : 10.
David fell, through the flesh.   2 Sam. 11 : 2–4.
Peter fell, through the devil.   Matt 16 : 23.

FIRE FROM HEAVEN.

Denoting acceptance of sacrifices.

Gen. 15 : 17.   Abraham.
Lev. 9 : 24.   Altar of burnt offering.
Judges 6 : 21.   Gideon.
1 Kings 18 : 24–38.   Elijah.
1 Chron 21 : 26.   David.
2 Chron. 7 : 1–3.   Solomon.

TRANSFIGURED — TRANSLATED — TRANSFORMED.

Christ —

 Was *transfigured* on the mount.   Matt. 17 : 2.
 Was *translated* at His ascension.   Acts 1 : 9.   Compare Heb. 11 : 5.

We —

    Are *translated* at conversion. Col. 1 · 13.

    Are being *transformed* by sanctification. Rom. 12 : 2.

    Expect to be *translated* at His coming 1 Thess. 4 : 16, 17.

    Shall be *transfigured* when we see Him. 1 John 3 : 2.

JUSTIFICATION.

By God, the *author* of it. Rom. 3 : 26.
By Grace, the *source* of it. Rom. 3 : 24.
By Blood, the *ground* of it. Rom. 5 : 9.
By Faith, the *principle* of it. Rom. 3 : 28 ; 5 : 1.
By the Resurrection of Jesus, the *acknowledgment* of it. Rom. 4 : 25.
By Works, the *manifestation* of it   James 2 : 21–25.

Sin is, —	*Jesus Christ is,* —
Folly. Ps. 38 : 5.	Wisdom. 1 Cor. 1 : 30.
Darkness. Col. 1 : 13.	Light. John 1 : 9.
Poison. Num. 21 : 6 ; Ps. 58 : 4.	The Antidote. Num. 21 : 9 ; John 3 : 14, 15.
Sickness. 1 Cor. 11 : 30.	Health. Mal. 4 : 2.

God wants as a sacrifice our persons. Rom. 12 : 1.
                     our property. Phil. 4 : 18.
                      our praises. Heb. 13 : 15.

MARY AT THE FEET OF JESUS.

    The prophet, teaching her. Luke 10 : 39.
    The priest, comforting her. John 11 : 32.
    The king, anointed by her. John 12 : 3.

Sin — past, present, and future — recognized and provided for : —

Past. — If we say that we have not sinned, we make Him a liar. 1 John 1 : 10.

Present. — If we say that we have no sin, we deceive ourselves. 1 John 1 : 8.

Future. — If any man sin, we have an advocate with the Father. 1 John 2 : 1.

FAINT NOT.

In prayer. Luke 18 : 1.
In confidence. 2 Cor. 4 : 1.
In hope. 2 Cor. 4 : 16.
In work. Gal. 6 : 9.
At tribulations. Eph. 3 : 13.
In well-doing. 2 Thess. 3 : 13.
Under chastening and rebuke. Heb. 12 : 5.

IT IS THE PRIVILEGE AND DUTY OF —

The Lord's people (Matt. 1 · 21 ; 2 Cor. 6 : 16), on
" " day (Acts 20 · 7 ; Rev. 1 · 10), to gather around
" " table (1 Cor. 10 . 21), to eat
" " supper (1 Cor. 11 · 20), in remembrance of
" " death (1 Cor. 11 : 26), discerning
" " body (1 Cor. 11 : 29), until
" " coming (1 Cor. 11 : 26), all linked together in
" " name (Matt. 18 : 20).

"BUT FOR A MOMENT."

> The hypocrite's joy. Job 20 : 5.
> The Lord's anger. Ps. 30 : 5.
> The liar's tongue. Prov. 12 : 19.
> Our light affliction. 2 Cor. 4 : 17.

WHEN YOU HAVE CROSSED JORDAN,

Beware of idolatry Deut. 4 · 15–24.
Be not unequally yoked with unbelievers. Deut. 7 : 1–3.
Beware lest thine heart be lifted up. Deut. 8 : 11–18.
Be separate. Deut. 18 : 9–14.
Be honest and upright. Deut. 19 . 14.
Be courageous. Deut. 20 : 3–4.
Destroy the Lord's enemies. Deut. 25 : 19.
Give the firstfruits to God Deut. 26 · 1, 2.
Love and obey the Lord. Deut. 30 : 20.

God working *for* us. 1 Sam, 14 . 6.
God working *in* us. Heb. 13, 21 , Phil. 2 : 13.
God working *by* us 2 Cor. 5 : 20.
God working *with* us. Mark 16 · 20; 2 Cor. 6 : 1.

OUR DWELLING PLACE.

1. "One thing have I desired of the Lord, that will I seek after; that I may *dwell* in the house of the Lord all the days of my life, to behold the beauty of the Lord, and to inquire in His temple." Ps. 27 . 4.
2. "He that *dwelleth* in the secret place of the Most High shall abide under the shadow of the Almighty." Ps, 91 : 1.

3. "Lord, thou hast been our *dwelling-place* in all generations." Ps. 90 : 1.

"PUT ON THE WHOLE ARMOR OF GOD."

Eph. 6 . 11–17.

The girdle of truth (for service). "I am the truth." John 14 : 6.

The breast-plate of righteousness (for the affections). "The Lord our Righteousness." Jer. 23 : 6.

The sandals of the preparation of the gospel of peace (for walk). "He is our peace." Eph. 2 : 14.

The shield of faith (for temptation). "The author and finisher of our faith." Heb. 12 : 2.

The helmet of salvation (for protection). "The Lord is my salvation." Ps. 27 : 1.

The sword of the Spirit, which is the word of God (for defence). "The Word was God." John 1 : 1.

"*Put ye on the Lord Jesus Christ.*" Rom. 13 : 14.

CHRIST ON THE MOUNT OF OLIVES.

The triumphal entry. Luke 19 : 29, 37.

Weeping over Jerusalem. Luke 19 : 41–44.

Prophetic teaching. Matt. 24; 25.

The night watches. Luke 21 : 37 ; 22 : 39.

The agony in the garden. Matt. 26 : 30.

The ascension (the last spot upon which He stood). Acts 1 : 12.

The coming again (the next place on which His feet shall stand). Zech. 14 : 4.

HEBRON.

The place of Separation.   Gen. 13 : 18.
The place of Worship.   Gen 13 : 18.
The starting point for Victory.   Gen. 14 : 13.
The place of Communion.   Gen. 18 : 1, 33.
The place of Promise.   Gen. 18 : 10, 14.
The place of Intercession.   Gen. 18 : 23–32.
The place of Conquest.   Joshua 10 : 36, 37.
A city of Refuge.   Joshua 21 : 11, 13.
The place of Weeping.   2 Sam. 3 : 32.
The place of Union.   2 Sam. 5 : 1.
The place of Anointing.   2 Sam. 5 : 3.
The place of Sovereignty.   2 Sam. 5 : 5.

NO DIFFERENCE.

Condemnation.— "There is no difference: for all have sinned and come short of the glory of God." Rom. 3 : 22, 23.

Salvation.— "There is no difference . . . for the same Lord over all is rich unto all that call upon him." Rom. 10 : 12.

THE CUP.

1. *The cup of wrath*, which all deserve.   "For in the hand of the Lord there is a cup, and the wine is red ; it is full of mixture ; and he poureth out of the same ; but the dregs thereof, all the wicked of the earth shall wring them out, and drink them." Ps. 75 : 8.
2. *The cup of salvation*, offered to all.   "I will take the cup of salvation, and call upon the name of the Lord." Ps. 116 : 13.

3. *The cup of blessing*, for believers. "My cup runneth over." Ps. 23 : 5.
4. *The cup of suffering*, which all must drink. "But Jesus answered and said, Ye know not what ye ask. Are ye able to drink of the cup that I shall drink of?" Matt. 20 : 22.
5. *The cup of consolation*, also for believers. "Neither shall men tear themselves for them in mourning, to comfort them for the dead, neither shall men give them the cup of consolation to drink for their father or for their mother." Jer. 16 : 7.
6. *A cup of refreshing*, which all may give. "And whosoever shall give to drink unto one of these little ones a cup of cold water only, in the name of a disciple, verily I say unto you, he shall in no wise lose his reward." Matt. 10 : 42.
7. *The cup of communion and testimony*, for believers. "After the same manner also he took the cup, when he had supped, saying, This cup is the new testament in my blood : this do ye, as oft as ye drink it, in remembrance of me. For as often as ye eat this bread, and drink this cup, ye do shew the Lord's death till he come." 1 Cor. 11 · 25, 26.

The great outlet of sin is the tongue ; the great inlets of temptation are the ear and the eye ; but of the whole body the heart is mistress. Therefore let grace rule the heart, and the whole man shall be subject.

TWO SIFTINGS.

Christ fans to get rid of the chaff. Matt. 3 · 12.
Satan sifts to get rid of the wheat. Luke 22 : 31.

AT HOME.

Judgment escaped. Ex. 9 : 19.
Work sifted. Haggai 1 : 9.
Labors ended. Luke 17 : 7.
With the Lord. 2 Cor. 5 : 8.

CHRISTIAN PROGRESS.

Onward. Ex. 40 : 36.
Forward. Ezek. 1 : 9–12.
Not backward. Jer. 7 : 24 ; 15 : 6.
Upward. Eccl. 3 : 21, Prov. 15 : 24.
Still upward. Ezek. 41 : 7.
Godward. 1 Thess. 1 : 8.
Homeward. Isa. 14 : 17 (margin).
Heavenward. Acts 1 : 10.
Toward the mark. Phil. 3 : 14.

WHO IS MY NEIGHBOR ?

The one who needs my help. Luke 10 . 29.
The one with whom I can share the lamb. Ex. 12 : 4.

There is a great difference between sin dwelling, and reigning in us It dwells in every believer, but reigns in the unbeliever.

God has two thrones, one in the highest heavens, the other in the lowliest heart.

The blood alone makes us safe. The Word alone makes us sure.

We are, as to our bodies, in Egypt:
" " " experience, in the wilderness:
" " " faith, in the Holy Land.

THE LAMB OF GOD.

On the altar. John 1:29.
On the throne. Rev. 5:6.
In eternity. 1 Peter 1:19, 20.

THE JOY OF THE LORD.

The shepherd's joy over his sheep. Luke 15:5, 7.
The seeker's joy " the piece of silver. Luke 15:9.
The father's joy " the prodigal. Luke 15:24.
The purchaser's joy " the treasure. Matt. 13:44.
The healer's joy " the cleansed ones. Jer. 33:9.
The Creator's joy " His works. Ps. 104:31.
The sower's joy " the sheaves. Ps. 126:6.
The father's joy " his wise child. Prov. 23:24; 17:21.
The king's joy " the willing people. 1 Chron. 29:9-17.
The Master's joy " His disciples. John 15:11.
The bridegroom's joy over his bride. Isa. 62:5.

"*Enter thou into the joy of thy Lord.*" Matt. 25:21.

SIMILES OF UNION BETWEEN CHRIST AND THE BELIEVER.

As father and son. John 17:21.
As Adam and the race. 1 Cor. 15:22.
As food with the body. John 6:56, 57.

As stones in a building. Eph. 2: 20–22.
As a vine and its branches. John 15:5.
As the body and the head. Eph. 4:15, 16.
As bride and bridegroom. Eph. 5:31, 32.

SEVEN CHANGES.

A changed mind. Repentance.
" " heart. Regeneration.
" " life. Conversion.
" " standing. Justification.
" " relationship. Sonship.
" " service. Sanctification.
" " body. Glorification.

FOUR TYPICAL MEN IN GENESIS, AND THEIR BRIDES.

Adam (human nature): his bride part of himself.
Isaac (death and resurrection): his bride fetched by the Holy Spirit.
Jacob (the servant): his bride the fruit of his labor.
Joseph (the head of his brethren): his bride nearer to him than his brethren.

ON THE MOUNT OF OLIVES.

Compare: —

David weeping over his rejection by Jerusalem. 2 Sam. 15: 30.

Jesus weeping over His rejection by Jerusalem. Luke 19: 41.

David foretelling his return. 2 Sam. 15: 25.

Jesus foretelling His return. Matt. 24; 25.
David contemplating his habitation. 2 Sam. 15 : 25.
Jesus contemplating the temple. Mark 13 : 3.
David wont to worship there. 2 Sam. 15 : 32.
Jesus wont to resort thither. Luke 22 : 39.
David's servants sharing his rejection. 2 Sam. 16 : 6.
Jesus' servants sharing His rejection. John 15 : 20.
David forbidding his servants to take vengeance. 2 Sam. 16 : 9, 10.
Jesus forbidding His servants to take vengeance. Matt. 26 : 51–53.
David's reward for his faithful servant. 1 Kings 2 : 7.
Jesus' reward for His faithful servant. Luke 22 : 25–30.

Contrast: —

A sorrowful procession. 2 Sam. 15.
A joyful procession. Luke 19 : 35–38.
David cursed by Shimei. 2 Sam. 16 : 5–8, 13.
Jesus kissed by the traitor. Luke 22 : 47, 48.
David's servants on his right hand and on his left. 2 Sam. 16 : 6.
Jesus forsaken by His disciples. Mark 14 : 50.
Shimei cursing as he went. 2 Sam. 16 : 13.
Jesus blessing as He went. Luke 24 : 50.

Never was there a lock of soul-trouble yet, but there was a key to it in God's word.

"Blessed be the God and Father of our Lord Jesus Christ " —

Who hath blessed us. Eph. 1 : 3. **Past.**
Who comforteth us. 2 Cor. 1 : 3, 4. **Present.**

Who hath begotten us again unto a lively hope. 1 Peter 1 : 3. Future

CHRIST'S SHORTEST ANSWERS.

"Go." Matt. 8 : 32.
"Come." Matt. 14 · 29.

NEW YEAR'S DAYS.

Atonement. Ezek. 45 : 18.
Cleansing. 2 Chron. 29 : 17.
Obedience Ezra 10 : 17.
Starting on a journey. Ezra 7 : 9.
Worship. Ex. 40 : 2.
Fears removed. Gen. 8 : 13.
The word of the Lord came. Ezek. 29 : 17.

Keep away from places where people say to you, "I did n't expect to see *you* here !"

THE TENDERNESS OF GOD.

As a father pitieth. Ps 103 : 13.
As a mother comforteth. Isa. 66 · 13.
As a hen gathereth. Matt. 23 · 37.
As an eagle fluttereth. Deut. 32 · 11.
As a nurse cherisheth. 1 Thess. 2 : 7.
As a shepherd seeketh. Ezek. 34 : 12.
As a refiner sitteth. Mal. 3 · 3.
As a bridegroom rejoiceth. Isa. 62 : 5.

HOW TO UNDERSTAND THE SCRIPTURES.

1. Pray earnestly for divine illumination. Ps. 119 : 18.
2. Meditate devoutly on the truths revealed. Ps. 119 : 97.
3. Inquire honestly, with a readiness to do the will of God when revealed. Acts 8 : 31–38.
4. Compare scripture with scripture. 1 Cor. 2 : 13.

A change of heart in regeneration is, —
1. Essential. Man may be saved without friends, money, honor, but not without the new birth. John 3 : 3, 5.
2. Thorough and universal 2 Cor 5 : 17. "All things are become new."
3. Above nature. It is by the power of the Holy Spirit. Eph. 1 : 19.

A SCRIPTURAL SUM.

The text for the following Scriptural sum may be found in 2 Peter 1 : 5–7. It is as follows : —

  Add to your faith, virtue.
  Add to your virtue, knowledge.
  Add to your knowledge, temperance.
  Add to temperance, patience.
  Add to patience, godliness.
  Add to godliness, brotherly kindness.
  Add to brotherly kindness, charity.

Answer. — For if these things be in you, and abound, they make you that ye shall be neither barren nor unfruitful in the knowledge of the Lord Jesus Christ.

THE LORD'S PRAYER.

1. *Our Father* — believers are children. John 1 : 12, 13 ; Gal. 3 : 26 ; 1 John 5 : 1.
2. *Hallowed be Thy name* — believers are worshipers. John 4 : 23 ; Phil. 3 : 3.
3. *Thy kingdom come* — believers are subjects. Luke 12 : 32 ; 22 : 29, 30.
4. *Thy will be done* — believers are servants. John 12 : 26 ; Rom. 6 : 16 ; 1 Peter 2 : 16.
5. *Give us our needful food* — believers are beggars. Matt. 7 : 7–11 ; John 14 : 13, 14.
6. *Forgive our trespasses* — believers are sinners. Rom. 7 : 21 ; 1 John 1 : 8, 9.
7. *Deliver us from evil* — believers are saints. Rom. 1 : 7 ; 1 Cor. 1 : 2 ; 2 Tim. 1 : 9.

SEVEN VOICES OF JESUS.

Shepherd's — "Follow me." John 10 : 27.
Master's — "Occupy." Luke 19 : 13.
Saviour's — "Come unto me." Matt. 11 : 28.
Teacher's — "Learn of me." Matt. 11 : 29.
Bridegroom's — "Open to me." Songs of Sol. 5 : 2.
Friend's — "I will sup with him." Rev. 3 : 20.
Physician's — "Wilt thou be made whole?" John 5 : 6.

BIBLE SIGNALS.

Danger : "The wages of sin is death." Rom. 6 : 23.
Caution : "Try the spirits whether they be of God." 1 John 4 : 1.
Safety : "Christ Jesus came into the world to save sinners." 1 Tim 1 : 15.

Protection : "The Lord shall preserve thy going out and thy coming in." Ps. 121 : 8.

Theodore Monod said : "After all, *obedience* is the best commentary on the Bible. *Do*, and you will *know*."

JESUS CHRIST, A SAVIOUR OF ALL CLASSES.

1. *The Astronomer* — Christ, the Bright and Morning Star. Rev. 22 : 16.
2. *The Baker* — Christ, the True Bread. John 6 : 32.
3. *The Botanist* — Christ, the Plant of Renown. Ezek. 34 : 29.
4. *The Builder* — Christ, the Foundation. Isa. 28 : 16. Christ, the Chief Corner Stone. 1 Peter 2 : 6.
5. *The Carpenter* — Christ, a nail fastened in a sure place. Isa. 22 : 23.
6. *The Electrician* — Christ, the Light of the world. John 8, 12
7. *The Farmer* — Christ, a Corn of Wheat. John 12 : 24.
8. *The Florist* — Christ, the Rose and the Lily. Cant. 2 : 1.
9. *The Geologist* — Christ, the Rock of Ages. 1 Cor. 10 : 4.
10. *The Herbalist* — Christ, a Cluster of Camphire. Cant. 1 : 14. Christ, the Root of Jesse. Isa. 11 : 10.
11. *The Horticulturist* — Christ, the True Vine. John 15 : 1.
12. *The Lawyer* — Christ, the Testator or Covenanter. Heb. 9 : 16, 17.
13. *The Merchant* — Christ, the Pearl of great price. Matt. 13 : 46.

14. *The Physician* — Christ, the Balm of Gilead. Jer. 8 22.
15. *The Sailor* — Christ, a refuge from the storm. Isa. 25 : 4.
16. *The Shepherd* — Christ, the Lamb without blemish and without spot. 1 Peter 1 : 19.

FIVE "IFS" TO BEWARE OF.

1. "If thou wilt." Luke 5 : 12. Doubt of divine willingness.
2. "If thou canst." Mark 9 : 22. Doubt of divine power.
3. "If I may." Matt. 9 : 21. Doubt of personal fitness.
4. "If it be thou." Matt. 14 : 28. Doubt of divine word.
5. "If the Lord would make windows in heaven." 2 Kings 7 : 2. Doubt of divine providence.

SEVEN-FOLD REJECTION OF CHRIST.

His own *World.* John 1 : 10.
" *Nation.* John 1 : 11.
" *Country.* Mark 6 : 4.
" *City.* Luke 4 : 29.
" *Kindred.* John 7 : 5.
" *Elders and chief priests and scribes.* Luke 9 : 22.
" *Disciple.* Mark 14 : 71.

www.ingramcontent.com/pod-product-compliance
Lightning Source LLC
Chambersburg PA
CBHW011950150426
43195CB00018B/2881